THE GA
OF
JU-JITSU

by

TARO MIYAKE AND YUKIO TANI

Includes 9 1 Illustrations
Drawings by George Morrow

Edited by
L.F. Giblin and M.A. Grainger

THE JAPANESE SCHOOL OF JU-JITSU

Table of Contents

DEDICATION

PREFACE

It is the aim of this book to show how two or three keen people can get most of the exercise and all the fun of Ju-jitsu without the aid of a school or instructor. Their progress may be slower and their methods not strictly correct; but the game need be none the worse nor its benefits lessened.

Many people may be attracted to a game such as this for particular reasons of their own. Some, whose business may lie in uncivilized countries, may merely require a practical means of self-defence. Some may be seeking health—not the timid health that is content to avoid sickness, but the health that is alive and rampant, a benediction in itself.

Others may desire the postponement of old age; nature does not demand that a man should be a mass of fat and atrophied muscle at fifty. (Take the outskirts of new countries, where men do varied athletic work with the fire of the footballer, a score of years after their London brothers have begun to hesitate over stepping off a bus in motion.)

Others may have in view the increased efficiency of work, the saving over sickness, the help to national defence.

But, in general, the case for this, as for any game, rests on the natural desire everyone has for fitness of body and ability to use it to best advantage in every circumstance, from hanging to a strap in a train to climbing the Matterhorn, and on the keen pleasure that comes from making and keeping it.

In modern life the games that are wanted must fill many conditions. They must be quick games, so that much may be done in half an hour, they must demand little space and no complicated apparatus; they must be possible in the middle of a town, indoors or out, by gaslight or daylight. Above all (unless the doctor and the schoolmaster are to drive people to them), they must have a natural attraction.

Hitherto there have been several games more or less of this nature. Take boxing as an example. It may have faults; it may depend too much on natural physical advantages; it may be dull at the beginning, and men may feel a touch of shame at taking it up as novices after boyhood—yet few will be found to deny that it is an admirable pastime. Nevertheless, boxing is seen to have the great defect—it does not attract the general public. It holds a certain number of enthusiasts; the rest make professions, dabble a little, find it strangely difficult to spare time—and drop it. Only one who has been concerned with the promotion and running of boxing clubs can tell how difficult it is to keep up their membership. Boxing has been fairly tried as a popular game, and (sad it is to say the thing!) found wanting.

Cricket and football, rowing, and the rest have made their place, have gained their bold upon our affections, and this fact would outweigh a thousand technical defects. But the boy who plays them comes sooner or later to town, and this dear half of his life must die. The town-bred boy—and this in town life is the bitterest thing of all—never gets this natural inheritance. And so, these games fail—for lack of opportunity—and men decay.

At this crisis Ju-jitsu enters. Technically it has all the virtues. It fills all the necessary conditions for a town game admirably. As physical training it has been particularly blessed by the most eminent medical authority for the all-round development that it aims at. Compared to boxing, progress is more immediate and continuous, and the interest is richer; in this respect it stands to boxing as chess to draughts. It supplies in very exact measure the element of contest, of intimate struggle, of fight-to-a-finish, that good exercise requires. This is particularly where boxing fails. The artificial restriction of gloves is not enough—the boxer may still get more knocked about and damaged than he likes; and one might as well agree not to run too fast in a race as to introduce a convention against hard hitting.

In Ju-jitsu practically no restriction is necessary. Man-to-man as God made you (usually with the addition of a jacket), you may fight it out to an inevitable finish; defeat when it comes is absolute, and the beaten man rises without strain or bruise ready to try again. This is the peculiar glory of i t.

In general, perfect fitness for one game does not carry with it fitness for another. Half an hour's high-jumping may mean a couple of days of soreness and stiffness for the man who can row half the day without fear of discomfort to follow. Every new game finds new muscles to exercise, new forms that the body must take. Only Ju-jitsu includes them all. It sets out to find the limit of movement in every direction, and those limits, as we shall see, are the locks which end Ju-jitsu contests. Because there is no continuous call on one set of muscles to cause over-development, deformity, and slowness; because quickness, quickness of movement and quickness of thought, is the persistent aim of the player; because perfect suppleness must be a conscious ideal with the beginner until it has become a second nature—therefore it is that Ju-jitsu helps all other forms of bodily activity and hinders none, and in Ju-jitsu we may seek and find the common basis of all athletic excellence.

With all this glory-garland of essential merit, Ju-jitsu—in England—must undergo the supreme test. Will it attract and please? Will it be found good fun? There are all the reasons why English people should play the game, but will they really do so?

So far (in the past year) some thousands of people have shown keen interest, as spectators, in the demonstrations given by the Japanese; some hundreds have begun the game themselves, and more are beginning. To an enthusiast the outlook would seem full of hope. But such tests are not enough; years must pass by before our questions can receive their answer. Meanwhile, Ju-jitsu is on its trial as an English game.

—THE EDITORS

NOTE—We hope that readers of this book will write and tell us when they find the descriptions wanting in clearness. We shall be very happy to answer questions and to receive suggestions. The subject has been a difficult one to put on paper, and we are much indebted to our colleagues, Messrs. J. Hirano, S. K. Eida, and Shozo Kanaya for help in this task.

TARO MIYAKE
YUKIO TANI

IN the four months that have elapsed since the publication of the first edition, Ju-jitsu has made visible progress in popularity. Cambridge has, naturally, taken the lead in the recognition of a new and valuable game; the enthusiasm of the University Ju-jitsu Club has been most gratifying. Charterhouse School , and the Royal Military Academy at Woolwich have both been undergoing instruction, and here and there (at such places as the Staff College and Oxford) and classes have been formed.

Last winter, in writing the Preface to this book, we deleted, at the last moment, various paragraphs dealing with the Ju-jitsu game for women— under the impression that feminine ideas were not yet sufficiently advanced to permit interest in any woman's game involving real physical exertion. We have been agreeably surprised to find that Newnham College has taken keenly to Ju-jitsu, and that Girton (as we understand) is on the point of forming a class for its study.

The Admiralty having made a grant for the purpose, the instruction of the Navy in Ju-jitsu began (October 1st) both at the School of Physical Training at Portsmouth and at Whale Island.

—THE EDITORS

TARO MIYAKE   YUKIO TANI

ADMIRAL KAMIMURA ON JU-JITSU

"However expert a man may be in the technical points of a Naval education, his service counts very little in time of war if he lacks presence of mind. The training in Ju-jitsu not only develops a man's physical power and agility, but it also tends to make him resourceful in meeting all kinds of emergencies and surprises. . . . When I took the cadets abroad on a navigation cruise, I found those who were experts . . . were the most efficient and capable. Their physical development and their mental activity make them able to stand hardships much better than ordinary men. My impression has been further strengthened by the present war. I would recommend not only naval men, but all young men to devote some hours of their time to learning. . . . The indirect benefit will be great in all walks of life."

PRACTICAL COURSE

We will now offer advice for the guidance of those who begin Ju-jitsu without an instructor.

There must be at least two pupils, but more are an advantage, that there may be someone to watch and criticize.

With the help of Chapter XIII on Apparatus, get ready to begin. Read Chapters I, II, III, and IV to the end of Throw 1.

Then practise the falling exercises you have read. Practise Throw 1 first roughly as a falling exercise, and then carefully for its own sake. Let each man in turn allow himself to be thrown. This will require two or three practices.

The next two practices should be given to learning Throws 2 and 3; do them first slowly, with great care to get the style correct.

Then mix the first three throws in a continuous practice, moving slowly about, each of you trying to give opportunities, not to avoid them. Continue this till you have a clear picture of the opportunity for each throw, and can do it without much thinking about it.

You are now ready for free practice.

The hints on page 14 will tell you how you ought to move—what to do and what to avoid doing with your legs.

Bearing these in mind, practise the first three throws freely.

Do this always for a few minutes before each practice.

As soon as you begin free practice with the three throws you have learnt, your mind is at liberty to tackle groundwork.

Read the Introduction to Groundwork, page 37.

Then begin the chapters on Locks; read the general remarks, and the description of Neck-lock 1, then practise it.

Then have a free struggle on the ground, starting from a fall, trying for the neck-lock you have learnt, and guiding your attempts by the general remarks in the Introduction to Groundwork.

That makes one lesson in groundwork.

In succeeding practices, add the other neck-locks, one by one, and then the leg-locks; you will see which are the most important.

When you have mastered some or all of these, begin the arm-locks.

These require a good deal more formal practice before you can use them effectively in a contest.

When you have been through the locks in this way, and learnt to use some at least of them practically, you should begin to put some system in to your groundwork.

Turn to Chapters VII and VIII on the Standard and Hold-down Positions. Work through these positions carefully, trying the various devices of attack, defence, and escape there described; test them thoroughly, critically, believing nothing until you have tried it well. Try also any other devices you can think of, and test them thoroughly. Meanwhile continue to practise the locks until you have a practical command of all of them. At any time you like after beginning groundwork read Chapter V, on the stomach-throw; practise the falling exercises a little everyday; and when you can do the complete breakfall exercise properly, try the stomach-throw. Add it, when it is mastered, to your free practice throws.

At a later stage you can try the more advanced throws. These you will find a good deal harder, and you need not be surprised if it is a long time before you bring oft one of them practically in free practice.

A complete practice, after the preliminary stages, will therefore be made up of these parts:

(1) Free practice standing-work, using familiar throws.

(2) Free practice groundwork; using familiar locks.

(3) Working out of standard positions with experiments.

(4) Formal practice of unfamiliar locks.

(5) Formal practice of unfamiliar throws.

(6) Formal right-handed practice of things that come more easily left-handed, and vice versa.

Every practice should include (1) and (2), and at least one of the others.

Miyake's Throw
The man's legs are pushed up into the air, and
then his body is rolled off the thrower's thigh

CHAPTER I
PRELIMINARY NOTIONS

What is Ju-Jitsu

You are going to play Ju-jitsu.

You are clad in (at least) a jacket, and stand facing an opponent, who wears a similar garment (see Chapter XIII on Apparatus). Your object is to maneuver him, *without using your strength*, into such a position that he is helpless and must give in.

The General Principle

Consider this phrase "without using strength." It is not exact because some strength must be used; it means practically "with as little strength as possible." If you use more strength than the weakest has at command, it is bad Ju-jitsu.

As a beginner you will find that you can overpower another beginner by using more strength than he does; but until you learn not to do so you are preventing yourself from learning to use more scientific methods. You must practise each particular throw or lock until you can do it "without using your strength."

In general, your first object will be to put your opponent on the ground; then you will continue the struggle there until one of you is compelled to give in.

Division of the Subject for Teaching purposes

It is convenient, then, to divide up the game into Standing-work and Groundwork, and to begin by learning a little of the first before attempting the other. There is in this way less burden on the beginner's memory.

Bear in mind, however, that the division is arbitrary. In practice, groundwork follows a throw instantaneously. When you throw, you want to put the man to the ground against his will in such a way that you have an advantage in continuing the contest. It would be quite permissible for him to go to the ground voluntarily in such a way that he would gain the advantage in the next stage of the struggle. Being first to the ground is not of necessity a point against you.

1

When you are thrown, you must again remember that groundwork ought to follow; and therefore, even when practising throws alone, you should get in the habit of gathering yourself at once into a good defensive position—on your back, with knees bent up, feet in the air, facing the enemy (see Fig. 32).

No rules for Experts

Throughout this book, for the sake of clearness, we shall generally very definitely, "Do this or that, put one hand here and one leg there," and so on. These directions are not to be taken as arbitrary rules. They are descriptions of one way in which the thing aimed at may be done.

Best methods not most useful to the beginner. Doctors disagree

Every good player will have his own way of doing them, and these ways will vary a good deal. Nor is it of necessity the best way that we have described. The best way often requires a suppleness or agility which is not common. We have tried to choose the most useful method for Englishmen of ordinary activity who are giving to Ju-jitsu the time and thought proper to a good game—not to a profession. Some difference of opinion is to be expected. Competent critics may say, "I don't do it that way; I prefer such-and-such a way." The point cannot be decided finally as yet; we have not played the game long enough in England.

Peculiarities of build useful

Our directions are, then, to be taken as suggestions; they describe possible methods. From their study and practice the pupil may get a practical and useful knowledge of the principles which should guide his movements. Then let him vary them as much as he pleases, and find out the methods most suitable to his own build and activity. Every man has some particular physical advantage, some joint that he can bend more freely than others, some movement he can make more quickly, some abnormal length or shortness of a limb. These personal characteristics he must find out and use. It is this building up of one's own personal system of Ju-jitsu which makes the special and lasting charm of the game.

These remarks hold true of all Ju-jitsu; they are particularly applicable to groundwork. There is no great room for differences of method in the simple throws; but groundwork has infinite variety, and always offers a fruitful field for experiment to the enterprising student.

The pupil will ultimately choose those methods which suit him best. But he must not be in a hurry; he must give them all a fair trial.

The lazy man

It often happens that he learns to do a few movements easily and without thought; and then in the stress of contest, particularly in ground-work, he relies on them entirely, and uses no others. This, of course, is wrong; he must be able to use a number before he is in a position to select. Therefore, he must practise as simple exercises those which he finds difficult until they become easy; and when he finds he is very apt in contests to use one particular lock, let him for a while bar out this lock, so that he is forced to use others.

Handicaps

Notice, by the way, that this barring out of particular locks is a very useful handicap to enable players of different skill to meet on level terms, whereby that great attraction of the game is not lost—the demand on both sides for the last ounce of endurance, activity, and skill.

Right-handed and left-handed

Every throw and lock and movement in groundwork can be done in two ways—according as you begin the movement with the right foot or the left foot, the right hand or the left hand, and so on. We describe one way without mention of the other. The description can, of course, be altered for the other case by reading left for right and right for left throughout. Both ways must be practised; they are of equal importance. The pupil will lose a great deal by being tied down to one side; it takes away half of his opportunities, and it is very apt to happen on account of his eagerness to pass on to new things.

The way actually described and figured below is generally the one which comes rather more easily to a right-handed man; but often the choice is quite arbitrary.

CHAPTER II
FALLING

The prejudice against falling and its unhappy consequences

Before you are thrown you must learn how to fall. Consider for a moment the strange dislike that people have to falling down. Probably you have that dislike yourself. You think it undignified and dirty. On Ju-jitsu mats these reasons vanish, but you still object to falling. It is now because you think you must fall on some projecting joint, and hurt it and get shaken up inside as well. Mere delusions! But while you nurse these delusions you will shrink from falling; every part of you will try to keep off the ground as long as possible, and the unhappy part (almost of necessity a joint) which hits the ground first gets the whole concentrated blow, and an internal shock is nearly certain to follow.

The true principles of falling

The reasonable course is obvious. Instead of avoiding the ground, try to hit it with as many square inches of surface as possible, all at the same time; turn your body and limbs suitably, so that the parts that hit the ground are not the bony parts, but the fleshy parts—of which the most useful are the palm of the hand, the sole of the foot, and the muscle-pads of the arms and legs. Try to sleep on a hard floor, and you will soon see how it is possible to rest your body, from head to foot, on muscle-pads. We will now show you how to fall on muscle-pads.

The Breakfall

The muscle-pads that will stand (with comfort) the greatest shock are those of the palm and forearm. Use these as much as possible, and strike the ground hard with palm and forearm at the very moment that the rest of your body strikes the mats.

At this same instant there should be a sudden stiffening of all the muscles, so that the arm becomes of one piece with the body, and takes on its pads a large part of the shock of falling. This is the simplest and most effective way of **breaking fall**.

5

Now for the best way to learn how to use the muscle-pads, so as to make falling as easy and as comfortable as sitting on a chair. (The principle is the same in both cases.)

Take these exercises in the following order:

Falling Exercise 1—Beating Mats

Position 1 — Lie on your back, head raised, knees bent, feet flat on the mats, arms stretched out not quite close to the side, but making a small angle with the body.

Position 2 — Raise the left arm, loosely bent over your body, so that the hand, palm upward, is toward the right shoulder; at the same time lift the right foot well into the air, so that the leg is nearly straight.

You are now in the position of Fig. 1. Bring the left arm back to the first position with a smack (slap the mats crisply with palm and forearm as hard as you can, and don't stiffen the muscles till the moment of striking); at the same time hit the mats with the flat of your right foot (do not pound on the heel), the knee, being well bent and the muscles. suddenly stiffened at the moment of striking.

Fig. 1—"Beating Mats" The dotted lines show where the arm and leg strike the ground

Repeat this till you can do it well, hitting hard and all together. Then practise the same with right arm and left foot.

Then make these movements alternately, raising the right arm and left foot the very moment the left arm and right foot hit the ground.

6

Judge by the crisp, loud noise: bang, bang, bang, bang, bang. When you are in good tight condition and do this well, **a quiver runs** right through the body from the strokes, and the body even lifts a little off the ground.

Falling Exercise 2

Tie a rope to a wall (or, better, a post or pillar) strong enough to support your weight, so that you can hold on to it at any height from two to four feet above the mats.

Lie on the mats (as in position 1 of the first exercise) with your left shoulder nearly under this rope; reach up and catch hold of the rope with your left hand and raise yourself on your right leg by it, lifting your left leg and right arm in readiness to strike the ground as in Exercise 1. Fig. 2 gives your position at this stage. Let yourself go, turning towards your right side as you fall, and "breaking fall" with right arm. You come down as in Fig. 3.

Fig. 2—Falling Exercise #2
You have raised yourself by pulling on the rope

When first attempting this exercise, raise yourself only a few inches; as you improve, keep on increasing the height (as far as you can comfortably), and so you are led to the next exercise—

Fig. 3—Falling Exercise The arm breaking the fall

Falling Exercise 3

Stand beside the rope, holding it in your left hand at about four feet from the ground. As in Fig. 4, throw the left leg forward in the air, let the right knee collapse, and fall backwards (using the pull on the rope to turn your body so as to fall almost on your side), breaking fall hard with your right arm, as in Fig. 3.

You will find it not very easy to fall nicely in this way. It is not necessary to be able to do so before attempting the throws in the next chapter. But it is useful to try it a few times first and then to practise it in the intervals of trying the throws.

The best way to improve your falling, when you have someone to practise with, is to treat Throw 1 in the next chapter as a falling exercise. Let one man try to throw and the other try to be thrown, not minding whether the motions of the throw are correct or not, but concentrating attention on the fall. Do this repeatedly from a standing position until you have learned to fall properly without thinking about it. Be careful always to let go, early in the fall with the hand that is going to be used to "break fall." There is a second reason for this—namely, that you do not want to bring the other man heavily on top of you.

8

Fig. 4—Falling Exercise #3 Throwing yourself

     Fig. 5 shows you most of the possible faults in falling: no muscle-pads used, no breaking fall with arms or legs, both arms clinging to the other man, and, worst of all, the whole shock coming on one unhappy point of the body. Some throws require different methods of breaking fall; these we shall postpone until they are needed.

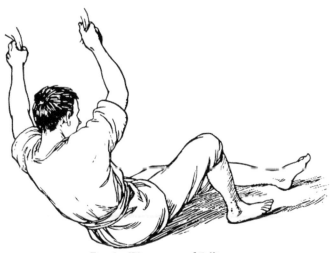

Fig. 5—Wrong way of Falling

CHAPTER III
STANDING WORK

The Throws

There are a great many different ways of upsetting a man by Ju-jitsu, and most of them are much too complicated to learn from a book. But those which are used most frequently are comparatively few and fairly simple. These few "throws" (they ought to be called upsets) we shall explain with very great detail.

Learn a few throws well

The few throws with which we shall deal form only a small part of the resources of the expert Ju-jitsu man; but they are quite enough for the ordinary person, even if he devotes the whole of his time for exercise to the game. For a good many years, certainly, a man will more profitably and pleasantly spend his time in exhausting all the possibilities of skill and quickness in respect to these simple methods than in learning complicated and more artificial new ones. Skill and quickness in seizing the opportunities for these simple throws and in escaping from your opponent's attempts can be developed almost without end. It should be some consolation to the ambitious to know that some of the best Japanese experts in Ju-jitsu, though familiar with a large number of complicated tricks, practically in serious contest depend on special skill and quickness in no more than three or four of the seven throws described in this book.

Moreover, with this material a keen man will naturally invent for himself combinations and developments which, while perhaps not so ingenious as the standard Ju-jitsu ways, may be just as useful to himself; for it must be remembered that Japanese methods have been invented for the typical Japanese build, and the methods most suitable for a heavy, long-legged Englishman have yet to be found out. This problem we leave almost as a duty to those of you whose ingenuity (unfettered by Japanese instructions) has no other assistance than our own inspiring words.

The throw in general

Suppose that you are walking along and come to an unexpected step down, without noticing it. The chances are that you fall; at any rate, you come down on your foot so shaken and unsteady that the least thing will upset you. That is the chance the Ju-jitsu man is looking for. You take a step forward; he can't cut away the floor under your feet to make a step down; but just as your forward foot is touching the ground, he can tip it up with a very quick movement of his own leg. You are bound to go forward, it is too late to draw back, and there is, for the moment, no foot to come forward on to (because it has been kicked into the air). For the moment you are unsteady, and the least pull sideways may upset you before you have time to get the kicked-away foot back to support you. Now you have had a real Ju-jitsu throw: the man has not used any force; he has merely caught you in a position where it was easy to upset your balance, and taken advantage of it.

This is very easy to talk about; but of course it wants a quick eye to see the chance and quick limbs to take it; and when you are on the look-out, the other man must have eye and limbs very quick indeed in order to be able to throw you that way.

Here we have had one very simple way in which a Ju-jitsu man throws another. There are a great many positions in which a man is unsteady, and the Ju-jitsu man learns them and how to take advantage of them in another, and how to avoid them as much as possible himself. And besides those that he learns he probably thinks out some more for himself. Of those he learns some do not suit his build, and he does not bother much about them; and others do suit his build, and these he practises a good deal, and is particularly on the watch for them. For some throws it is good to have long legs, and for some it is good to have short ones, and so on.

You have already learned to fall well enough to make the practice of the first few throws enjoyable.

To begin the game

You are on the mats with your instructor X.

We are going to suppose all through that you are playing with X, a man who knows Ju-jitsu, because it makes description easier. If you are both new to the game, you will each in turn play at being X.

12

The grip

The first problem is **how to engage.**

You will find that X takes hold of you with a light, firm grip with the fingers of both hands. He holds you at points a little below the level of his shoulders, because that gives him the strongest pull. (Compare the almost level arms in rowing.)

He chooses points as far apart as possible, because that gives him the greatest leverage when he wants to turn you round.

He likes to have at least one hand in contact with your body, (not your arm), because he may want to get a firm purchase on your body (and your arm would give from the shoulder.)

To satisfy all these wants, he will probably take your right-hand collar with one hand and the sleeve of your left arm (just above the elbow) with the other, as in Fig. 6.

Fig. 6—How to Hold
There must be no stiff, contracted grip

This is not a fixed rule; he may alter his hold to one more suitable for some particular purpose; but this arrangement is the one most generally useful. You had better take hold of X in the same way.

13

If you have seen two Ju-jitsu men at practice, you will have noticed that they start off at once skipping up and down the room, holding one another. You may have wondered why they do so. It comes about in this way. When X takes hold of you, he throws his weight in such a way as to pull on you in some direction without putting his balance in danger. Now two things are open to you: to hold back and resist, or to give to the pull and move in that direction. If you do the first, you find that you cannot resist much without putting your own balance in danger; so that if X were suddenly to cease to pull, your own force of resistance (thus left unbalanced) might unsettle your equilibrium, and X could easily upset you. It does not pay to play the resistance game with X, because he knows how to put on more pressure than you without endangering his balance. The safer course, then, is to give to his pull and to move with him, and so preserve your own balance. In fact, it always come to this—that the better man can lead the other about if he wants to, and that the best thing the other can do is to give way to the motion and wait for a chance.

Nothing, then, is to be gained by trying, to stand still, so players usually start off moving at once, sometimes one directing the motion, sometimes the other. What they do and don't do with their feet, you will learn gradually.

General rules for deportment

Meanwhile, this advice may help you:

(1) Keep the body upright on the hips—this is the first principle of good balance; avoid like the devil the bent position of Fig. 12.

(2) Keep the arms supple and a little bent; you will find that straight arms lay you open to horrible catastrophes.

(3) Keep the legs straight but not stiff; don't prance up and down on bent knees; glide your feet; avoid high-stepping.

(4) Never cross your legs; good players do so with inferior ones, but they take liberties. Keep your feet well apart; never let them stay near to one another.

(5) Finally, keep your body soft all over; every muscle supple and expectant.

CHAPTER IV
SIMPLE THROWS

Two people play—you and X (a Japanese).

In all throws it is most important to seize the exact opportunity for bringing off the throw with the least effort and the greatest effect.

This we shall simply call opportunity.

FIRST THROW

You are learning: X will throw you several times, and then— you will try to throw X.

Figs. 7, 8, 9, 10 show how X does it.

The opportunity for X to upset you comes as you are making a step towards him, just at the moment your left foot (say) is reaching the ground and your weight is coming on to it (Fig. 8).

Fig. 7—From this safe position you step forward

Fig. 8—The Leg-blow, just as your foot reaches the ground

15

Fig. 9—The Side-pull upsetting you   Fig. 10—Your Fall

SECOND THROW

Now X shoots out his right leg (stiff from the hip-joint down, with the toes stretched as far as they will go), and with a sharp side movement of the whole leg brings the under-part of his instep against the side. of your leg (just above the ankle) with a kind of pushing blow (Fig. 8), which lifts your leg well into the air.

Your weight was just coming to this leg, you miss the support you expected, and at the same moment pulling in with his arms X sends your body to his right with a twist of his hips and shoulders.

We hope you fall according to the instructions you have received on page 8—that is to say, you let go with the right hand, keep hold with the left long enough to turn your body, and fall almost on your side with a hard smack of right hand and forearm as your body touches the mats (Fig. 10).

Now X asks you to throw him; he offers you a leg in just the right position, and pauses to give you plenty of time.

You try to kick his leg away, and very probably his balance remains undisturbed.

Fault 1—Perhaps you kicked with a bent leg, and so there was no pushing strength in the blow (Fig. 11).

16

Fig. 11—Fault: leg bent

Fault 2—Perhaps you put your leg in too deep and struck with your calf.

Fault 3—Perhaps your blow was too slow—all push; or too sharp—a mere knock with push (that only affects X's temper).

Fault 4—Perhaps the leg-blow was correct, but you bent forward from the hips. You were stooping and bunched up and off your balance, and almost fell over yourself (Fig. 12). This bending forward is the **Fatal Error** in Ju-Jitsu.

Fault 5—Next, perhaps, you get the leg-blow right, and the body a trifle sloped back to get a steady balance—and still X does not upset.

Your pull is wrong; you are pulling with the right arm and pushing with the left. That merely twists X round without disturbing his balance. You want to move his body so that it is no longer right above the solitary leg that supports it. To do this you must pull in with the arms and swing the shoulders hard round to the right from the hips. Everything depends on this swing of the upper part of the body.

Fig. 12—The Fatal Error—bending forwards
Also the arms are stiff

Fault 6—If you fail now it is because your leg-blow and arm-pull are not at the same time. The pull is probably too late; X has already disengaged his leg when you pull.

When at last, having corrected all these faults, you make another attempt, you will be vastly relieved to hear X fall with a loud smack. (He makes the smack for his own benefit, but it is cheering to the vanity of the beginner.)

These, therefore, are the things to remember:

(1) Body must be straight—at moment of throw must be leaning a little back on the hips. It will continue naturally to lean yet further back as the leg-blow is made.

18

(2) Leg must move in one piece from the hip, straightened out to the farthest toe as if trying to reach as far as possible.

(3) Under part of instep must hook X low down on his leg to get maximum blow from you and maximum leverage on him. (His leg is the lever on his body.)

(4) Pulling with one arm and pushing with the other is useless. Both arms must pull the same way, rather to the right; the elbows tucked in close to the body and the pull as little down as possible.

The arm-pull must be accompanied by a strong twist of the shoulders as far round as they will go.

You can now do the first throw correctly; you must learn to do it quickly.

In actual practice X would make his leg "soft" as soon as he saw you were trying to use this throw, and his leg, when you kicked it up, would be no stiff lever (to help in upsetting him), but a limp limb which slipped away over your instep and was back to support him before his balance had been seriously disturbed. But every man must make his leg stiff for a moment just as he is putting his weight on it (and before his foot is quite firmly planted on the ground). This is the best opportunity; this is the moment you must try to seize (as you improve) with lightning rapidity. And another moment comes when the man is moving back just as he is about to withdraw the foot nearest to you. You must try to seize these moments without giving warning of your intention.

Now X upsets you again. X was on your left front. He placed his right foot a few inches outside your left and level with it (rather nearer than in Fig. 13).

He swung his hips and left leg to his right (Fig. 14), then with a return swing of hips and leg he kicked away your left leg from behind. The blow was delivered with a leg quite stiff from the hip (Fig. 15). It caught your leg a sharp blow from behind about the back of your knee. The tendons of your leg collapsed; your weakened leg was carried away into the air (Fig. 16). At the very moment your leg went, X pulled your body in with his arms and carried on the motion with a long swing round of his shoulders to the right. Then you fell round to his right side.

Fig. 13—Opportunity for Second Throw   Fig. 14—Swing round of hip

Fig. 15—Return Swing and Kick   Fig. 16—Side-pull upsetting you

20

Now you try to throw X.

Fault 1—At the first attempt you upset yourself. You were not close enough: no power at a distance (Fig. 17).

Fig. 17—Wrong way of trying Second Throw;
you are too much in front of X, and you have
not swung your hip around

Fault 2—Next you hooked X's leg with your own leg bent. No effective blow; and you nearly upset.

Fault 3—You merely tried to push X's leg away.

Fault 4—This time you kicked with the side of your leg on the side of his leg could not collapse from the side.

Fault 5—This time you did not swing your hips round so as to get position for the return swing. You tried to knock his leg away only using your leg.

Fault 6—This time the leg-kick was correct, but your pull was a mere jerk with the arms. You did not swing him round with your shoulders.

Fault 7—In trying to pull you bent forward and merely pushed X with your weight. The **FATAL ERROR** again.

Now at last pull and kick come together, and X upsets smack. Remember, therefore:

(1) Foot on which you stand must be not far from the side of X's foot with toe pointing out, and so

(2) Hip must pass close to his hip.

(3) Kicking leg must be stiff (feel your big toe stretched stiff).

(4) Kick must catch him from behind.

(5) Elbows, as you pull in, come close to sides; swing round of shoulders must be as long as possible.

(6) Avoid the FATAL ERROR.

(7) Kick-back must have the swing of the hips behind it.

Note—This throw is most effective when X is deep at your side. Your hip and leg are then already in position for the kick-back.

For example, you are moving backwards, and X is following you with the same direction of motion, but a little to your left front. You put down your right foot and pause a moment on it, before bringing back your left. As you do so, X may advance his left foot past your left, so that (owing to your pause) he comes up to your side. The step back with your left foot, which you have delayed for an instant, you now convert into the kick-back of this throw, and, with the proper arm-pull and shoulder-swing, X goes down. Here your hip and leg are already in position, so that the throw comes about instantaneously, without preparation. And X's motion helps the arm-pull.

THIRD THROW

Again, if you are at rest, X must be a little leaning forward on his left foot for the throw to come off easily. The arm-pull therefore comes, if anything, a little before the kick.

X upsets you by this throw. In Figures 18, 19, 20, you are the man in black socks.

You and X were revolving round one another. X came suddenly to rest; you were moving to your left (Fig. 18).

Fig. 18—Opportunity   Fig. 19—Your left leg prevented from moving

X leaned back; you wanted to move left leg to left front to support yourself. But before you could do so, X shot out his right leg as in Fig. 19, and held the ball of his foot firmly against your leg just over the knee-cap. He leaned further back, pulled in with his right arm, lifted with his left, and you toppled over his foot as in Fig. 20. You held on with your left hand, turned right over in falling, and came down with a right-hand breakfall.

Now you try to throw X this way: X wears the black socks.

Fault 1—Your left foot is in the wrong place. Its position is very important. Notice that, as in Fig. 19, it must be outside of X's right foot. Evidently it must be such a distance away that the ball of your foot will just reach X's left knee. To judge correctly the position of the left foot is the most important thing in this throw.

Fault 2—Your left toe is pointing as in Fig. 19. This is correct for the expert. You, as a beginner, had better plant your left foot with the toes turned in (almost at right angles to the correct position), because you can thus more easily turn your body.

Fault 3—The position of your right foot is wrong. It is in front of X's leg, and does not trip him; or it is too low, so that he can lift his leg over it; or it is too high, and stops X from toppling over.

Fault 4—Your pull is wrong: you do not lift with your left arm. Try to shift your hand and lift under X's armpit.

Fault 5—You are not leaning back enough. At the last moment of Fig. 20 you must lean well back—further than the photograph shows. Do not mind about your balance; you are bound to be unsteady after bringing off the throw. Fix your attention on upsetting X.

Fig.20—You topple over. X's Arm-pull is not shown well; he could not keep in position before the camera

Remember these points:

(1) Left foot to go well to your left, so that you can just reach X's right knee.

(2) Left toe turned to the right.

24

(3) Ball of foot over, and just over, X's knee.

(4) Right arm pulls in and down; left arm lifts.

(5) Body leans back; avoid the FATAL ERROR.

Escape

Escape from this throw either by swinging the leg round X's foot (Fig. 21), or by sending your body close in against X.

Fig. 21—Escape from Third Throw, bringing the body
well in, and swinging the leg round over the foot

This throw is difficult when you try it, from the proper position, without being in motion. The pull and lift with the arms is awkward. But if X has a circular motion round you, the difficulty goes. X's own momentum topples him over with very little help from your arms. The faster the motion the less the arm work.

Since this throw depends particularly on motion, do not try much from a stationary position. Practise it a great deal when you are both moving, remembering that everything depends on a correct position for the left foot. It is only by practice that you can learn to see, or learn to make, your opportunities for any throw—but more especially for this one.

25

CHAPTER V
FALLING AND STOMACH-THROW

Exercise 1

You must now learn to break fall when you pitch forward heels overhead.

Lie flat on your back .

Raise your legs and arms into the position of Fig. 22, rolling well up on to the shoulders with a swing.

Fig. 22—Break-fall Exercise

Swing back the legs, shooting them straight out. As you come over, arch the back and bend the knees a little, so that you come down as in Fig. 23, breaking fall smartly with flat feet and with both arms.

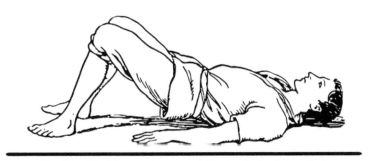

Fig. 23—The blow on the ground. Notice the back is arched

Your chief object is to let the feet and arms hit the mats exactly together, and take the shock instead of the bottom of your spine. This latter is very apt to hit the ground first with an unpleasant jar, so you must suddenly arch the back just before striking. Bend the knees smartly to get a good slap with the soles of the feet.

Remember:

(1) Let arms and feet strike together, so that only one noise is heard.

(2) Arch your back at the last moment.

(3) Slap with the soles of your feet smartly; do not pound on the heels.

This breakfall can only be used in special circumstances. The sideways breakfall that we shall now describe may nearly always be used when you are pitching forward on to your head. It is most important for you to practise it carefully, and you will find it not so difficult as you at first suppose.

Exercise 2 Breakfall exercise from a kneeling position

Settle in your mind that you are going to fall straight in front, along a line drawn on the mats.

Kneel down, and place your left forearm (palm upwards) flat on mats, and straight across the line.

Rest your head lightly on the mats in front of the arm; let it be well tucked in, with the face turned to the right.

Rise on your feet into position of Fig. 24.

Push off with the legs and go over, your left shoulder well rounded and tucked in. You scarcely come on it at all; you come over on to the part of the back just below it, where the dotted line begins.

Fig. 24—Break-fall Exercise. Pushing up from a kneeling position

At this moment the feet are straight in the air (Fig. 25), the head hardly touching the ground, the body and legs screwed a little to the right.

In going over (always in the direction of the line) the body is screwed a little more to the right. You come over on to your right hip, lying a little on your right side almost along the line.

Fig. 25—Going over. The pressure will come along the dotted line

29

You strike the mats as in Fig. 26, breaking fall with right hand and both legs.

Notice that in Fig. 26:

(1) The right leg is straight out, and strikes on the muscle-pads of calf and thigh and instep. The sole of the foot is turned to look upwards.

(2) The left foot comes flat on the sole, and is turned so that the knee may be bent as little as possible.

(3) The strokes of the flat left foot, the muscle-pads of the right leg and right arm must all be sharp, hard, and exactly at the same time. Judge by the noise.

Fig. 26—Final position of Break-fall. Notice the sole of the right foot is turned upwards

You may find this exercise hard to do correctly, because when you are in motion upside-down it is not easy to think of which way you ought to turn. You may get some help by lying down in the final position and trying to work yourself slowly back from there to the original position.

Thus, from the position of Fig. 26 you lift your legs over your head, keeping the head off the ground with rounded back. Roll back slowly, and notice as you go the points of your back where your weight rests. These points should start from the right buttock, cross the back slanting, pass the backbone about the middle, and finish up on the left shoulder-blade (see dotted line in Fig. 24). Stop when you have got back as far as this, reverse the motion, and break-fall again as in Fig. 26.

Try again and again until you can do this quickly without thinking; you are thus learning the turn of the body and the breakfall with legs and arm.

Then roll up with a little more force and go right over, coming more or less back into the position of Fig. 24.

Finally, practise the whole movement backwards and forwards. This teaches you the breakfall, but only from a kneeling position.

Exercise 3 Complete BreakFall

Now you are ready for the complete exercise.

Stand up, dive forward on to the mats, throw your legs over your head, and come down in the position of Fig. 26.

The motions are exactly the same as in the previous exercise, except that you start standing up and throw yourself forward.

Notice that:

(1) You stand with left foot forward, left shoulder dropped a little forward, and left arm ready bent.

(2) You aim for a point on the ground two or three feet in front of you.   That is where your forearm is to come.

(3) Head is turned a little to the right and rather tucked in.

(4) Heels must be thrown well up and left shoulder must be kept well rounded, so that the first part of your body to touch the ground is about the top of the shoulder blade.

(5) Forearm takes very little weight; head none at all.

(6) You must come down on the line you have drawn on the mats. Your body and legs must always keep the true direction when moving, in spite of the fact that your head and shoulders are turned towards the right.

Dive well forward

Do not be alarmed about your head. It is because they sunk the forward dive that beginners come over in a hunched-up position and sometimes jar themselves. As you gain confidence, try to dive farther and farther out. Then you may get a friend to lie under you and stomach-throw

31

you forward again and again. Finally, let your friend lie on the ground with his foot up as in the stomach-throw, and take a running dive right over him.

At first you will find that your body tried to come up into a sitting position at the moment of breaking fall. Resist this; put a sudden little stiffness into your body, so that instead of coming up it shoots several inches along the mats after the breakfall. It is worth your while to practise this exercise a good deal before making the least attempt at Exercise 4, otherwise you will get a very slovenly style.

The same as Exercise 3, except that instead of wasting the rebound from the breakfall, you allow it to carry you up on to your feet again. Take our advice, and leave this exercise alone until you can break fall properly.

FOURTH THROW

You have now learnt to come down comfortably when you pitch forward on to your head. X can therefore upset you by the stomach-throw (Figs. 27, 28, 29).

You were leaning forward , or pushing forward, or moving quickly forward, or holding X stiffly at arm's length.

The throw

X stepped in between your legs with his left foot; leaned back with all his weight hung on you (so that your body went more forward); put the sole of his right foot against your navel, with his knee tucked well up close to his body (more so than in Fig. 27), and fell backward on the mats. He bent the knee of his left leg sharply as he fell, so that his body came down close against the heel and well under you. Poised on his foot with your weight well forward towards his head, you pitched over in that direction (as in Fig. 28). X kept his right leg well bent as you pivoted over it, and finally off by suddenly straightening it (Fig. 29).

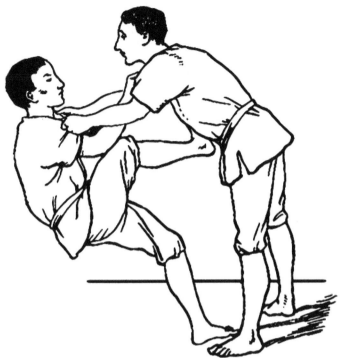

Fig. 27—First movement of the Stomach-throw.
The raised leg must not push

Fig. 28—Just going over. Notice that the man underneath is
not pushing with his leg

33

Fig. 29—The final push with the leg. If the leg pushes
before this moment, the throw will probably fail

Until you get accustomed to this throw X will be very careful to keep
hold of you, and thus let you come down comfortably (if you arch your back)
into the breakfall position of Fig. 23.

Afterwards he will let you pitch clear, and you must try the expert
method of falling shown in Figs. 25, and 26.

Now you try this throw on X.

Faults

(1) Your left foot is too far away; X can stop his forward motion.

(2) You have not bent your right leg sufficiently.

(3) You have not fallen close to your own heel; you are not under X
enough. In all these cases you only manage to push X away with
your foot; he does not get fairly on top of it.

(4) You give the little push with your right leg too soon. X is stopped
in his forward motion and may roll off sideways.

(5) Your foot is too soon; X parries by lowering his body.

(6) Your foot is too late; X merely falls on top of you.

Remember then:

(1) Knee of the leg that supports X must be well tucked in against your own chest. You must not push with this leg until the last.

(2) Body falls close up to the foot you were standing on.

(3) Body must fall and foot come up to X's stomach both at the same time.

This throw is the sure penalty for the Fatal Error and for Straight Important Arms Pushing Forward.

CHAPTER VI
INTRODUCTION TO GROUNDWORK

Locks

We have now considered the most useful simple throws. We go on to discuss the continuation of the contest on the ground. It has been already explained that this goes on until one man surrenders because he cannot go on struggling nor even lie still without the certainty of a broken joint, unconsciousness, or some other equally unpleasant penalty. These positions which end the struggle are called "Locks"; the most important ones will be found below, fully described and illustrated.

After a throw

What happens between the throw and the lock? At first sight, only a confused, aimless struggle; a welter of arms and legs whirling rapidly in strange contortions, with little respect for the injunction "breakDon't use your strength."

After a while you begin to see some reason; you notice that certain positions are constantly being aimed at which give particular advantages for attack or defence; you find that certain movements are carefully avoided and certain others are used freely; you find that strength is chiefly used to remedy defects in knowledge or skill.

At the best, groundwork cannot be described as systematically as standing work. There are too many possible positions; and the best players do the same thing often in different ways. What we can do is this:

(1) Collect a number of principles, to be constantly remembered, and a number of hints and general remarks of frequent application.

(2) Describe the standard positions above mentioned, showing some ways of reaching them, and some of the many possibilities of attack and defence which these positions involve.

(3) Describe the principal locks very fully, and indicate the most usual positions from which these locks follow.

Men are so accustomed to use their legs for nothing but standing, walking, and running, that when they are struggling upon the ground they only think of attack or defence with their arms. Now, the legs have much more strength than the arms, and use should be made of them.

It may be roughly said, Ju-jitsu groundwork is merely the proper use of the legs. Success depends on the activity and agility of the legs: the temptation to use the arms for everything must be fought against and conquered. Keep your bent legs between yourself and your opponent—and he can do you no harm. Wrap your legs around his body—and you have a master position for several locks. Clasp them round his neck—and he may surrender. Bring up a leg and push the man's head away; use a leg whenever you can.

The use of the muscles of the body must be encouraged; the body must lose all rigidity; it must be a limb. The hips must swing freely when the shoulders are held fast, the backbone must bend at every joint. You must be a wriggler, an eel, impossible to hold. Learn to wriggle by practising the writhing exercise given in Chapter VIII. Strength counts for more in groundwork than in standing-work. A great difference in strength makes some locks fail for the weaker man; and it is not so easy to turn a man's strength against himself. Even so, strength counts for much less than quickness, skill, or intelligence; and it remains equally true that it is only in so far as you avoid using strength that you have any chance of improvement.

Remember these general rules:

(1) Never turn your back.

(2) Use your arms as little as possible and your legs as much as possible.

(3) Avoid using strength.

(4) Use your head as a limb, and be ready to tuck it in tightly at any attack on your neck And above all—

(5) Get your knees between yourself and the other man, or get your legs round him.

(6) Conversely, avoid his doing the same to you.

Consider now the different positions of the man who throws and the man who is thrown.

The man who is *Down*, who is below the other, shall be **D**.

The man who is *Up*, who is above the other, shall be **U**.

What to do after throwing a man

What is **U** to do after he has thrown **D**?

(1) If **D** holds on to his jacket with one hand, **U** has a chance of winning at once by Arm-lock 1, which is described fully in the section on Locks, Chapter XI.

(2) Otherwise, **U** throws himself on to **D**'s body, as in Fig. 30, and tries either—

   (a) To straddle across him on his knees in a position of great advantage for attack, which we call Standard Position I, and discuss fully below; or

   (b) To lie across **D** in a position which is not particularly good for attack but keeps **D** down; such positions we call Hold-down Positions, and describe fully in Chapter VIII.

What to do after being thrown

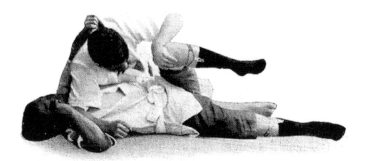

Fig. 30—After a Throw

What is **D** to do when he has been thrown?

(1) **D** will let go his hold of **U**'s coat the moment before his body hits the mat.

(2) He will bring his legs up, as in Fig. 32, and try to spin round in the same motion, so as to get his knees between himself and **U**, and so prevent **U** from getting into the straddle position or to a hold-down position.

If **D** succeeds in doing this, he takes away the advantage that **U** has gained from the throw.

Fig. 31—After a Throw. The thrower has come down into the Straddle Position

Then will follow a contest in agility and quickness between **U** and **D**, which will end in one of them gaining a distinct advantage.

Fig. 32— The man thrown must spin round into this position

Either—

i. U will get past **D**'s legs to the straddle or to a hold-down; or

ii. **D** will get a hold of **U**'s jacket with his feet still between himself and **U**, a position we shall call Standard Position II; or

iii. **D** will get his legs linked round **U**'s body; this we shall call Standard Position III.

Standard Position II

D is on his back with a hold of **U**'s coat, and his knees between himself and **U**.

This is what we mean by Standard Position II.

Fig. 33—Standard Position II, one of the best positions for D

This definition includes a good many slight variations of position. When **D** has one knee in; he can generally get two.

When he has his knees in, he can also get his feet up against **U**'s hips.

He can also slip his legs on either side of **U**, though he cannot of necessity link them behind **U**.

All these possible variations we group together as Standard Position II, because it is generally possible to pass from one to the other.

When **D** can link his legs round **U**, we get a new position, not included in II, which we deal with separately as Standard Position III.

41

Fig. 34—Standard Position III, one of the best positions for D

CHAPTER VII
GROUNDWORK

The Straddle Position

Standard Position I, from which **U** should win.

U, kneeling on the mats, grips **D**'s sides just above the hips with his legs. He keeps control of his own weight, not letting it rest idly on **D**, lest the latter should bunt him up suddenly with his hips. When **D** tries this sudden bunt-up, **U** grips tighter with his knees and clasps with his feet under **U**'s thighs.

On first coming into the position, **U** with his right hand gets a deep hold of **D**'s right collar. This is generally possible.

Fig. 35—Standard Position I, from which U should win.
Notice the fine opportunity for an Arm-lock

Fig. 35 gives the correct position. But if **U** has short legs, he will perhaps prefer the position of Fig. 36. In this he has thrown his weight on to the left knee, come up on the right leg, and secured a very deep hold almost at the back of **D**'s neck with the right hand.

The advantages of this are:

(1) **U** has a steadier balance.

(2) He is more in position for the swing round to lock **D**'s right arm.

The disadvantage is:

He leaves more space between himself and **D**'s body through which **D** may wriggle a knee or slip an arm.

Fig. 36—Some people prefer this form of
Standard Position II

U'S ATTACK—AGAINST THE NECK

Attack 1—The main attack is against the neck. (See Neck-locks 1 & 2).

Defence—**D** may guard this by putting both hands to his jaw (see Neck-lock Defence); but if he does so he can make no progress towards escape, and he also exposes himself to the forced arm-lock. But still he may parry **U**'s attempts for a while with his hands.

—AGAINST THE ARMS

Attack 2—The attack against the neck may be a feint to provoke **D** against to expose his arm . Under cover of this attack **U** works his left knee the arm; forward under **D**'s right shoulder, keeps **D**'s upper arm away from **D**'s side with his thigh, and steals his right foot out to the ground (it is already there in Fig. 36). Then suddenly clasping **D**'s arm, **U** sways his weight across on to the right foot. At this moment his left leg hoists itself from the ground, he returns his weight with a sharp push off the right foot, and the left leg sweeps round over **D**'s head as **U** falls on his back in the position of Arm-lock 2.

So much careful preparation may be unnecessary if only **D** exposes his arm enough. **U** may then simply clasp it, yank it more up by the sleeve, and swing round into the lock.

44

Without much hope, **D** may try to guard by keeping his right shoulder resolutely to the ground and the elbow-joint close to the side. Of course, he must be careful not to expose his arm by pushing at the upper part of **U**'s body.

Attack 3—If **D** clasps his hands to prevent the arm-lock, **U** may get his leg across more leisurely, pass his right forearm through the crook of **D**'s arm, and lean back to force the arm-lock, (see Arm-lock 3).

—AGAINST THE LEGS

Attack 4—If **D** keeps his knees bent, **U** can twine his legs under and against round them, pitch his body a little forward, and secure Leg-lock 3 (the "splits"). **U** cannot do this quickly, and at the first feel of **U**'s legs **D** should shoot out his own legs straight. He will be quite safe from this lock if he never allows his legs to remain idly bent behind **U**'s back.

Attack 5—**U** may attempt a bent arm-lock (see Arm-lock 6).

ESCAPES

The defence already described will not help **D** for long. He is in a desperate situation, and must make active attempts to escape.

The most favourable moment for escape is when **U** inserts. his second hand for the neck-lock. **U** has then an unsteady balance and can be easily upset. But **D** must not leave his neck exposed a moment too long. He must parry vigorously (without giving chances for an arm-lock), and then, when **U** has almost worked in his second hand, suddenly leave his neck exposed and upset **U** at once.

D may push with his hands at various parts of **U**'s body; this makes the only difference between one way of upsetting and another. The student should make experiments; perhaps he will find the following way the best.

Escape 1—When **U**'s right arm is uppermost, **D** will upset **U** to his own right side. It will be found that the choice of this side makes it easier for **D** to unwind himself from the neck-hold after upsetting **U**.

By pressing with his right hand into the crook of **U**'s left arm (or by pulling down on **U**'s left sleeve), **D** will draw down **U**'s left shoulder while he pushes up on **U**'s hip (or shoulder) with the other hand. He gives a hoist at the same moment with his left hip, and **U** goes over.

If **D** is not careful, or if he tries to roll over on top of **U**, he will probably roll between **U**'s legs, and he is in no better position than before, since **U** can go on locking the neck without interruption (see Standard Position III).

After upsetting U, D may unwind the neck-hold

Therefore, **D** must take advantage of the moment of upset (when **U**'s legs will be loose) to jerk his body back to the left away from **U**'s legs, and then to scramble round (face downwards) until he gets opposite **U**'s head. **U** may have kept his grip on **D**'s collar, but his hands are no longer crossed and **D** has unwound the neck-lock. **D** has now the advantage, and may secure Hold-down 4 with possible arm-lock to follow; he has also a chance of getting Hold-downs 1, 2, or 3, or he may possibly get into the straddle position.

U may say himself from upsetting

U may prevent this escape by getting his weight down very smartly on the neck-lock as soon as his second hand gets hold. It is a contest in quickness between the two, with the advantage on the side of **U**.

Escape by getting through under U's legs

Escape 2—If **U** is in the position of Fig. 36, the following escape is to be preferred.

At the moment of the neck-lock **D** inserts an arm under **U**'s stretched-leg, draws it to him, and hoists it round over his own head. As the leg swings on to **U**'s arms its weight breaks away the neck-lock grip of **U**'s hands, and **D** is free.

This also is a contest in quickness—whether **U** can tighten the lock or **D** throw him off first.

It is important to notice that neither this nor the preceding escape can be hopefully attempted until **U** has got both hands in for the neck-lock grip; yet **U** must not be allowed actually to get the grip. The upset must therefore be very carefully timed.

Wriggling a knee through between U's legs

Escape 3—**D** may heave up with his hips—getting a thrust off his legs, and at the same time push **U**'s hips away and up with straight arms. If **U**'s grip with the knees is weak, **D** may work a gap between himself and **U** through which he may bring a knee, and so wriggle in to a position of advantage.

This may "take some doing": it may require a quick rush of desperate attempts with pretended attacks on other parts, before **U** is caught in a moment of weakness.

D's Attack

Fig. 37—Standard Position II, from which D should win

Notice first the chances which **U**, by carelessness, may give to **D**.

Chance 1—Should **U**'s left hand rest on the mats by **D**'s side, **D** can pin it between his arm and side, and by pressing over with the right knee on **U**'s elbow secure an arm-lock. **D** will find that a switch of the hips to the right gives him a better position for pressing with the knee.

Again, if **U**'s hand comes anywhere on the upper part of **D**'s body, **D** can pin it with one hand and bring on the knee-pressure. This may sometimes cause sufficient discomfort to amount to a lock.

Defence—**U**'s defence is simply to keep his arms away from these dangerous positions.

Chance 2—If **U** is foolish enough to try to lock **D**'s neck in this position, he may forget himself and press forward. **D** can then throw him over his head by a sort of stomach-throw, and possibly come over himself as well into the straddle position on top of **U**.

Defence—**U** can put out an arm and prop himself. He should be always ready to let go a neck-hold suddenly.

Chance 3—If **U** tries to stand upright (perhaps with the intention of bumping **D** on the mats), **D** can let go, catch hold of both **U**'s ankles, pull them towards him, and push at **U**'s hips with both legs. **U** will go down on his back.

If **D** pulls the ankles well in, he may secure a double leg-lock at once, or possibly come over in to Standard Position I. But if **U** is active, he may escape altogether, and **D** will merely have lost his advantage.

Defence—**U**'s best plan, after falling, is to break **D**'s weak grip of his ankles, and to whip his legs up over himself out of harm's way.

Now, Attack 1 will only succeed when **U** is very unwary. Attacks 2 and 3 do not lead to much as a rule. **D**'s serious attack is as follows:

Attack 4—For arm-lock or neck-lock **D**'s wants **U**'s body to come nearer. He therefore pushes away **U**'s left knee with his right foot, so that **U** comes lower and perhaps even falls on the other knee.

(a) First **D** tries the neck-lock, getting his hands deep in while he is pushing the leg away. With a purchase from his left leg on **U**'s hip he can force **U**'s body close to his own. **U** either gets neck-locked or else pushes at the upper part of **D**'s body.

(b) If **U** pushes with an arm (suppose the right) at the upper part of **D**'s body, or if he tries to neck-lock, then **D** has an opportunity for the one-leg arm-lock (see Arm-lock 4). Fig. 38 shows the opportunity. **D** pins the right wrist, swings his left leg over across **U**'s throat or face, straightens his leg, and arches the back a little so that his hips come up against the elbow.

Notice that this lock comes most easily when **U**'s hand is well in at **D**'s neck. In other cases, **D** may need to yank the arm forward by the sleeve.

Defence—**U** must leave the upper part of **D**'s body alone.

Attack 5—We see that either (a) or (b) of the last section should prove effective. But **D** has another useful resource.

When **D** has pushed **U**'s left knee away, as in 4, he lets his right foot pass between **U**'s legs and over **U**'s left calf in order to keep that leg down.

Fig. 38—A fine opportunity for locking U's right arm

Then a push of the foot on **U**'s right hip, helped by the natural pull and push of the arms, will send **U** over sideways and **D** may come over on top and gain Standard Position I. Fig. 38a shows another upset.

Defence—**U** is bound to go over, but he must try to seize the moment of falling to wriggle in a knee between himself and **D**.

Fig. 38a—The Turn-over

From Standard Position II, D has passed one foot between U's legs. In the Fig., D is hoisting U's left leg with the top of his instep, while he pushes down U's right knee. The natural push and pull of the arms helps to turn U over.

U's escape

We see that there is no effective defence against **D**'s possible attacks, and no important counter-attack. **U** is in a thoroughly bad position, and his main thought must be to escape from it as quickly as possible. **U** must not be so foolish as to try to neck-lock **D**. He would be pushed away into the harmless position of Fig. 38, and would risk the one-leg arm-lock.

He must at all costs remember to keep his hands from the upper part of **D**'s body; he may push at **D**'s stomach or hips, or, with more safety at **D**'s knees. He had better give all his attention to one of the following methods of escape.

Escape 1—**U**, by pressing hard and suddenly at **D**'s knees, might break away **D**'s grip of his jacket, and then be free to attack on level terms.

He cannot do this if **D** has pushed his legs away; in any case he exposes his neck.

Escape 2—**U** may push on **D**'s knees, suddenly ease the pressure of **D**'s feet by shrinking back with his hips, dash both of **D**'s legs aside, and come in to a hold-down position.

Or, better:

U may move his left leg back so that **D**'s right foot slips down from the hip, then, dashing **D**'s left leg away as in Fig. 39, he may come in to **D**'s left side in a hold-down position.

Fig. 39—U escaping from Standard Position II, and
dashing in for a Hold-down

When **D** finds his legs thus dashed to the right, he may twist back on to his left side and whip over his right knee to fend off **U**. **U** may counter by pressing this knee down and jumping right over into a hold-down on the other side.

If **U** can only dash away one of **D**'s legs, he may still with luck manage to roll ii round the other leg and secure a hold-down.

Note—It is understood that **D** keeps a grip of **U**'s jacket in all these maneuvers. Otherwise **U** may tuck one of **D**'s feet under his arm, step through, and secure a standing leg-lock (sec Leg-lock 1).

Escape 3—**U** may get his arms between and under **D**'s legs, and drop his body between **D**'s legs. There are three things he may then do.

(a) He may clasp hands over **D**'s stomach (or grip **D**'s belt as far in front as possible) and hoist until **D** is stood on the back of his head.

The weight of **D**'s body drives his chin into his chest: a little additional pressure makes this a neck-lock.

(b) He may turn **D** on his side, one leg in the air. By hoisting the lifted leg overhead with one arm he may break away **D**'s hand-grip and can then slip up to **D**'s side for a hold-down.

(c) He may nuzzle his head under one of **D**'s legs and wriggle through to the side, breaking away **D**'s hand-grip as before.

In all these cases **U** must tuck his head well down and be quick. Otherwise **D** will snap his head in to the leg-squeeze neck-lock (see Neck-lock 5).

Standard Position III, from which **D** should win.

D has not only got his legs round **U**, but has also managed to clasp his feet together behind **U** (Fig. 40). This is a very fine position indeed. Read again what we have said about the Standard Position II, and you will see that most of it holds good for this position; with the difference that many things are now much easier for **D** and much harder for **U**. Notice that **D** does not have to push **U**'s legs away, because he is already in a very good position for the main attacks against neck and arm; while **U** can make but a poor defence,

Fig. 40—Standard Position III: D's legs clasped together around U

and his methods of escape from Standard Position II are no longer possible.

Escape 1—**U** might force **D**'s legs apart by pressing out at the knees.

Escape 2—**U** might manage to rise to his feet (lifting **D** with him), and then either force **D**'s legs down or make **D** leave by bumping him on the mats.

In either of these escapes **U** must first expose his neck to a lock. **D** will try to finish the lock before his legs are pushed away; **U** will try to escape from the legs so that he can circle round and "unwind" the neck-hold before it is too late.

A blow has been parried, the
striking arm seized and twisted
and the man is being thrown by
a Kick-back

CHAPTER VIII
THE HOLD-DOWN

What is a Hold-Down

D is on the ground; U is holding him with little effort in such a way that he cannot get up or even change into a new position as long as U is sufficiently on the alert. But D is not particularly uncomfortable, and is not obliged to surrender. This is therefore not a lock: it is a "hold-down."

The hold-down is useful for several reasons:

(1) It gives U a rest, while D may exhaust himself in struggling to escape.

(2) U is free to move into other positions: D is not.

(3) U can wait till D, in struggling, exposes himself to a lock.

(4) Sometimes a hold-down leads directly to some particular lock.

Hold-Down 1

A hold-down is most frequently used when U has just thrown D, or has got past D's leg defence and come in to his side. U must then have something he can do quickly before D's legs whip round between them: he generally begins with the hold-down of Fig. 41.

Fig. 41—First Position of Hold-Down 1

U has sprung in from D's left side and come down at right angles across D's body (Fig. 41).

(1) Left hand on the ground with arm hard against D's right hip.

55

(2) Right hand on the mats above **D**'s shoulder, and forearm exerting a disconcerting pressure against **D**'s jaw (some people say the fingers should grip **D**'s clothing).

(3) Knees extended wide, one hard into the armpit, the other against the hip. (Notice that **U**'s weight is not on **D**'s body, but on his own hands and knees.)

U obliged to change his position

This is not in itself a secure hold-down. If **D** writhes his hips with persistent vigour, **U**'s position will be disturbed. But **U** can at any moment fall from this into a new position, lying on his side with his weight on **D**'s body, one knee tucked up against **D**'s body, the other leg straight out at right angles.

There are a number of such useful positions, **U** using his arms in different ways and lying either on his right or left side. When **D** in his struggles gets near an escape, **U** must change from one of these positions to another, rolling from right to left or left to right as occasion requires, and throwing his weight now on **D**'s hip, now on his shoulder.

A few such simple movements will keep und er control the most frenzied efforts of **D**, but they must be well timed and well directed. Success, as always in Ju-jitsu, depends on quickness and judgment. **U** must also try to keep bis body soft, to avoid being thrown over by **D**'s strength. He must be a limp dragging dead weight at **D**'s side. **D** may clasp his chest and give a tremendous heave; but if **U**'s body comes limply the heave is all lost before it reaches his legs, and they do not fly over. Whereas if **U** had stiffened himself, **D** might have thrown him right over like a stick held at one end. Convince yourself by a trial.

There is one more caution for **U**: let him keep one leg straight out and always at right angles to **D**'s body.

Here are the two principal variations of Hold-down 1 (Figs. 42 and 43). Remember that the details will vary according to what **D** does with his arms and hips.

Fig. 42—Second Position of Hold-Down 1: Notice the elbow is on the ground

Second Position

From the position of Fig. 41, **U** may turn on to his right side and lie as in Fig. 42.

(1) Right thigh and knee hard against **D**'s side (closer than in the figure).

(2) Left leg stretched out at right angles to **D**'s body (or a little round towards the head, as in Fig. 42).

(3) Right elbow and forearm on the mats, hand gripping **D**'s belt; or round **D**'s right shoulder, gripping just below armpit, as in the figure.

(4) Left hand gripping **D**'s belt (or pressing on left hip).

(5) Head well tucked in, so that **D** cannot press up the chin or snap the bead away with his leg.

(6) Weight against **D**'s chest and chin.

Or, again, from the position of Fig. 41 **U** may turn on to his left side and lie as in Fig. 43.

Fig. 43—Third Position of Hold-Down 1: Notice the elbow is on the ground

Third Position

(1) Left thigh and knee hard against **D**'s side.

(2) Right leg straight out.

(3) Right hand gripping **D**'s right coat-collar (possible one-handed neck-lock).

(4) Left forearm flat on mats.

(5) Head well tucked in.

Hold-Down 2

This is not a very secure hold if **D** is strong and **U** is light, but it gives particularly good chances for three locks.

In the position of Fig. 44, notice that **U** can very easily get these from the position of Fig. 43 by shifting his whole body along towards **D**'s head.

(1) **U**'s left thigh is well under **D**'s left upper arm—as much under the shoulder as possible; knee projecting above the shoulder.

(2) Left arm round **D**'s neck as far as possible.

(3) Right hand holding **D**'s jacket to prevent the shoulder from working away.

Fig. 44—Hold-Down 2: Three locks possible from this position

If **U** can bring **D**'s straight arm, palm up, down across his thigh, he can clap his right heel over the wrist and secure Arm-lock 5.

If **D** resists the straightening, **U** can suddenly give to the resistance and catch the arm for the Bent Arm-lock 6. This is not a very good lock.

If **D** in struggling manages to throw his right leg round over **U** (in the hope of getting a purchase), **U** can hook the leg with his right arm, pass the hand on under to grip his own thigh, catch his left hand also on to his other thigh, and bend **D** round his back in the cradle-lock (see Neck-lock 6).

Defence—**D** must struggle and wriggle with cautious energy. Perhaps he may be able to clasp his arms round **U** and hoist him over.

Hold-Down 3

This is very secure, and may sometimes amount to a lock. It might occasionally follow on from Hold-down 2.

(1) Left arm round **D**'s neck with elbow on ground. As in many positions on the ground, the elbow on the ground has a very important effect in making the balance secure.

(2) Hands clasped and arms squeezing tight round **D**'s neck and shoulder.

(3) Head snuggled well down, pressing **D**'s upper arm against his jaw.

(4) Body out at right angles from **D**'s body.

(5) Legs somewhat spread.

59

Fig. 45—Hold-Down 3: U's head ought to be lower

Hold-Down 4

U secures this from behind D's head; the opportunity for securing it does not come very often .

(1) Arms under D's arms and gripping his belt, or they might be clasped together on D's chest.

(2) Legs well spread out.

(3) Weight well down on D when he struggles.

(4) Head well tucked down.

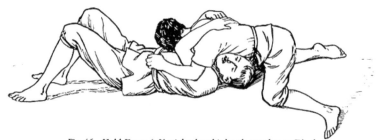

Fig. 46—Hold-Down 4: U might clasp his hands together on D's chest

When D puts his arms round U's neck—a very natural thing for him to do—he exposes himself to a forced arm-lock (see Arm-lock 3).

60

Writing Exercise

It is so very important for the beginner to get his body-muscles into good working order, and to get in the habit of making proper use of them, that we will describe here a writhing exercise that will help a good deal.

X lies flat, on his back, with his legs slightly bent at the knees. He then passes his right foot over so that it comes to the ground as far to the left as is convenient, while both shoulders remain on the ground (Fig. 47).

Next, without lifting the right leg, he draws the left leg sharply through under it. The moment the left leg has come through he throws it over (with a sharp screw of the hips) well to the right. It comes down in the same sort of position that the right leg had in Fig. 47. The moment the foot touches the mats the right leg is drawn through and thrown over, and so the exercise continues. The shoulders all this time are kept on the ground, and all the work of twitching the hips from side to side comes on the muscles of the lower part of the body.

Fig. 47—Writhing exercise: Shoulders must be kept on the ground

CHAPTER IX
INTRODUCTION TO LOCKS

It has been already explained that a lock is the end of a Ju-jitsu contest; a position for one man in which no course is open to him but surrender. The most useful locks are described below under the three headings of Neck-locks, Arm-locks, and Leg-locks, according to the part attacked.

These locks must be practised by themselves as exercise—both to get ease in using them in contest, and to get experience in the amount of strain which can be safely applied.

This point requires a little care; some locks applied with a rough jerk might injure a limb before the signal of surrender could be made.

(The signal of surrender is a double tap made with hand or foot on the mats or on the body of either combatant.)

The locks that require care are the arm-locks; in all of them the pressure must be applied gradually. The preliminary movements may be done as rapidly as possible, but the bending of the forearm beyond its natural play must be done slowly and carefully.

To snap back the arm with a jerk, amounts to Foul Play.

Never resist when the arm is nearly straight

On the other hand, the man locked must also take a little trouble. He must not resist the straightening of the arm to the last moment, because the power of resistance diminishes so rapidly, as the arm is straightened, that the arm will go suddenly with a jerk. Once the arm has begun to give, he had better let it go easily, and try to escape by wriggling his body.

Again, when he has once been thoroughly convinced by experience that he cannot long resist the pressure, there is no use in holding out to the last moment on every subsequent occasion; he will soon learn to recognise when the lock is properly applied, and should then tap the mats at once.

These cautions are particularly to be remembered in arm-locks.

In neck-locks there is no danger; and it is often necessary that the actual pressure should be sharply applied; but violence is unnecessary.

63

In general, if pupils will go slowly at first, try the locks carefully a few times, and afterwards use common sense, there is little danger of accident of any kind.

NECK-LOCKS

If a hard knob is pressed into the side of a man's neck directly below the ear, it causes no acute discomfort; but a feeling of helplessness comes over his mind, which ends in unconsciousness, if the pressure be continued.

Again, if a hard edge be pressed against the front of the throat—against the Adam's apple—it causes a choking feeling with rather acute discomfort, which will also end in unconsciousness. The aim of a neck-lock is to exert one of these two pressures. Since neither of them is instantaneously effective, the man must be prevented from changing his position, so as to escape the pressure; there are, therefore, two things to do—one to get a secure hold, the other to exert an effective pressure. In accordance with the general principles of Ju-jitsu, ways of doing both these things must be found which do not require the exertion of any great strength.

We will describe six of the most useful methods of neck-lock. For convenience, we will call the man who locks, the Victor, **V**, and the man who is locked, the Loser, **L**.

Neck-Lock 1—The double-handed neck-lock

Fig. 48 shows a common application of the lock. **V** is in the straddle position (Fig. 35) on top of **L**. With arms crossed, he takes hold of **L**'s collar as deep as possible, almost at the back of the neck; the hands should be not more than four inches apart, palms outwards.

He pulls on his hands, forcing the elbows out until the forearms almost come into line; to do this his body must come down with all its weight till it is close to **L**'s, breast to breast.

Pressure against the side of the neck

At the same time, he turns his palms upwards with a screw of each forearm; so as to drive the bony edges on the thumb-side of the forearm (particularly the knob at the wrist) in to the sides of **L**'s neck. **L** cannot move or twist to escape the pressure because he is held between **V**'s legs.

This, then, is a lock.

Fig. 48—Double-handed Neck-lock

Theory

V used no great strength. By getting his hands in deep, he was able to use the forearms as levers (as a nutcracker would act if its handles could cross), merely by letting his bodyweight force down the elbows. It is necessary, therefore, that **V** should be able to move his body down close to **L**'s, chest to chest. If anything stops that, ,the lock cannot be made.

These are the essential points:

(1) Hands deep.

(2) Thumb-sides of arms against **L**'s neck.

(3) Bodies together, breast to breast, at the finish.

(4) **L**'s body unable to move without taking **V**'s with it, still breast to breast.

There are other positions besides "the straddle" in which these points can be observed, and the lock consequently obtained. For example, **V** may be underneath in Standard Position II or III.

In practice, **V** gets hold with one hand first, say, the right. It is generally possible to get this in very deep. Then he passes the left hand under the right arm, and tries to work that in also. He may not get it in as deep as he would like, but the extra depth of the other hand may make up for this, and the lock, if not so neat, be fairly effective.

(Notice that one hand, in this case the right, may be described as nearest to **L**'s chin; we shall want to speak of it presently.)

According to the exactness with which the above conditions are satisfied, the lock will vary from one that produces. almost instant surrender to one that a strong-necked man can endure for any time without great discomfort—one which is therefore no lock at all. **L** must be careful, then, not to be bluffed into surrender.

Defence against the lock

L may make direct opposition to the neck-lock in several ways. He may try to stop **V** from getting a hold or from getting his elbows down to the lock (1) by holding his own chin, (2) by pushing away **V**'s hands, or (3) by pushing upon **V**'s elbows. Nothing of this sort is of much use; it only serves for a time. Of course, **L** must not push at the upper part of **V**'s body, because that exposes him to an arm-lock (see Arm-lock 2).

There is only one sound defence for **L**.

He must free his body from **V**'s hold, seizing the moment when both of **V**'s hands are busy getting a deep hold on his collar. The most useful methods of doing this are shown in the escapes from Standard Position I. Suppose now that **L** has freed his body from **V**'s legs, but is still held in the neck-lock grip by **V**'s crossed arms. He cannot push **V** away without risk of an arm-lock. He must make **V** uncross his arms; he must "unwind" the neck-lock by circling round **V**'s shoulders with his body and legs.

If he circles one way, he loosens **V**'s grip; if he circles the other way, he tightens it; and in a contest he has no time for mistakes. He must therefore find out by practice which way he should move.

Unwinding the neck-lock

This rule may help him. If **V**'s right hand is nearest his chin, he must circle to his right; if **V**'s left hand is nearest, he must circle to his left, until the pressure is released.

This generally means half a circle.

When **V** straddles **L** in the position of Fig. 36, the lock may be conveniently varied in this way.

V gets his right hand in deeper than usual on account of his position; he inserts his left as before under the right, but is content to get hold of the front of **L**'s collar.

V puts on the lock as before; but it is now practically a single-handed lock. The pressure comes from the edge of the right arm across the front of the neck; **V** only pulls with the left arm to get a purchase off it.

V may be upset at any moment, and as he can obtain the necessary pressure for this form of the lock only when he is above **L**, it is therefore much less useful than the general form of the lock.

Neck Lock 2—Single-handed neck lock

When **L** is on his back and **V** over him in the straddle position, **L**'s neck can be locked with one arm.

Fig. 49 shows the method of the lock.

V puts his right hand in deep as before, and with his left pins **L**'s right arm out on the mats. He brings the bony edge of his right forearm across the throat, and bears down with his weight on it. He pushes with his left arm off **L**'s wrist, so as to bring the weight of his body fairly above his right elbow. At the end of the lock **V** is more forward, more to his right, and closer to **L** than is shown in the figure.

Notice that the pressure falls on the front of the throat, the Adam's apple, and is acutely uncomfortable with a choking sensation.

Fig. 49—Single-handed Neck-Lock. L is prevented from turning by the purchase on his arm

Theory

A very small twist of **L**'s body would take the strain off a one-handed neck-lock; therefore, **L**'s body must be securely held down. In the two-handed lock simple twisting of the body does not loosen the lock. It makes one hand tighter as it loosens the other.

This position with one arm pinned out on the mats is the only one which holds **L** rigidly enough for the single-handed lock to be effective. At the same time, the thrust off the wrist is of great value in increasing the pressure which it is possible with one arm to bring on the throat.

Notice that sometimes when **L** has left no gap at his throat for the insertion of the forearm edge **V** may compel surrender by screwing over **L**'s jaw.

Neck-Lock 3

This lock is so easy and effective that any man who turns his back to the enemy in Ju-jitsu may almost consider himself beaten.

In this lock the bony edge of the forearm is pressed firmly against the throat, while **L**'s head is driven forward over it by pressure from The neck behind.

As in the last lock, a twist of the body would release the pressure, and it is therefore essential that **L** should be held so that he cannot turn out of the lock.

By using different forms of this lock, it can be applied to **L** in a number of positions—standing, sitting, kneeling, flat on his face, or lying on his back with **V** under him; the only condition is that he should have his back turned to **V**.

Standard Method

The most complete form of the lock is shown in Fig. 50. **V** has his right arm round **L**'s neck, gripping the collar as far round as possible, the bony edge of the forearm against **L**'s throat. He passes his left arm under **L**'s left and brings the forearm over so that the palm of the hand rests on the back of **L**'s head. A firm contraction of the right arm and a pressure on the back of the head with the left drives in the forearm-edge and closes **L**'s throat.

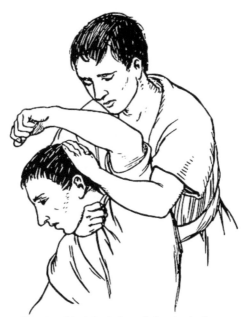

Fig. 50—Neck-lock from behind: ideal way

The position of **V**'s left arm keeps **L** exactly in his place; he cannot turn without taking **V** along with him. It is not, however, possible, as a rule, for **V** to get his left arm into that position .

Other Methods

(a) **V** puts his left hand over **L**'s left shoulder and grasps his own right hand (in the usual cup-and-ball manner). He does not now need a collar-hold. A contraction of the arms will drive the right forearm into **L**'s throat if the back of the head is pushed forward with the right shoulder. In order to do this, **V** must be able to get his shoulder on a level with **L**'s head. This position gives a fairly firm hold of **L**, but not so firm as the standard one. It has this advantage, that no hold of the collar is required.

(b) The method commonly employed is that of Fig. 51. Here the hold is given by the legs; **V** has them linked round **L**. The collar-hold and the right arm are exactly as in the standard method; the left hand is pushed directly against the back of **L**'s head. In this position the left hand may be pushed away by **L**; **V** may avoid this by using the elbow of his bent arm instead of the hand.

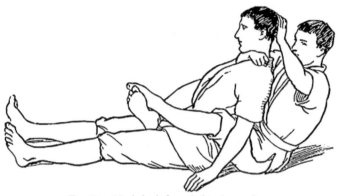

Fig. 51—Neck-lock from behind: usual way

Neck-Lock 4--Chancery

This lock is shown in Fig. 52.

V has his right fist clenched in the hollow of his left hand (cup-and-ball hold, shown clearly in Fig. 57), and the bony edge of his arm against **L**'s throat. **V** makes sure that his hands are firmly joined, forces back his right shoulder, and arches his back strongly. The forearm comes against the front of **L**'s throat as in Neck-lock 3. (**V** is not likely to be allowed to pass his arm round **L**'s neck: he should try rather to raise his elbow and to let **L**'s head slip under it.) If **L**'s body can follow his head freely as **V** arches his back, the lock will fail. Therefore, for an effective lock, **V** must keep **L**'s body down; that is, in general, he must have his legs linked round **L**.

Fig. 52—Chancery Neck-lock
Action on the neck is just the same as in the Neck-lock from behind

70

Neck-Lock 5—The Leg Squeeze

If V can get his legs linked round L's neck, he has L in a very awkward position (Fig. 53). The hard bones of V's knees press into L's neck. By straightening the legs V can make the pressure very severe. It is not easy to direct the pressure to particular points of L's neck, but wherever it comes, it is effective enough to produce a lock. The expert is perhaps inclined to regard it as a little crude, but its effectiveness is certain; the beginner should get a good deal of pleasure and profit from its use (on another).

Fig. 53—The Leg-squeeze
V will let go of the jacket and straighten his back when giving the final squeeze

The opportunities for it are too varied for detailed mention. Whenever L's head stick out with a clear neck there is an opportunity. The defence for L is simply to cultivate the habit of keeping his head tucked in, when he is within reach of V's legs.

Neck-Lock 6—The Cradle

From Hold-down 2 or from a failure to secure the thigh-and-foot arm-lock, V may have a chance of getting the cradle-lock (Fig. 54).

His left arm is round L's neck: he must catch hold of his own left thigh. Then, at a moment when L, in struggling to escape, brings his left leg near to him, V must tuck it under his right arm, and pass his right hand his own right thigh.

Now V begins to bring his knees together, and L gets stretched round his back until the strain on the neck compels surrender.

It is quite useless to try to do this lock by the strength of the arms.

The hands must hold the thighs, and it is the strength of these latter that stretches L round.

71

Fig. 54—The Cradle: V puts on the strain by closing his legs

CHAPTER X
LEG-LOCKS

Leg-Lock 1—Standing Leg Lock

The attack is directed against the very tender spot at the base of the calf.

When **L** is on his back keeping off **V** by his leg defence, **V** may find an opportunity to seize **L**'s left leg, and to tuck it under his right arm, with the bony edge of the forearm against the base of the calf. Before **L** can thrust him away with the other leg, **V** must step through between **L**'s legs, bringing his left foot over to **L**'s left side (and so turning his back to the battering of **L**'s free leg). Now **V** may place his other hand on the captured leg, clasp his right hand on to his own arm, arch his back, and so drive his forearm into

Fig. 55—Standing Leg-lock
Pressure against the base of the calf—a very tender spot

73

the base of **L**'s calf. This will cause instant surrender. Fig. 55 shows the position before **V** has begun to arch his back.

Another Way

If **V** had found it more convenient to tuck the leg under his left arm, he might have stepped over into the position of Fig. 56. Should **L** escape the lock in this position by turning over on his face, **V** should still keep his grip on the leg, and secure the lock in the new position.

Leg-Lock 2

Fig. 56—Another position for the Standing Leg-lock

V finds it convenient to catch **L**'s left leg under his left arm and to lie down to the lock. He has passed the edge of his arm round under the base of **L**'s calf, brought it up tight and caught the ball of his fist in the cup of his right hand.

He now sinks down with left knee well bent (so that his body comes close to the heel), and while doing this throws his right leg over L's thigh. The moment his body reaches the ground he throws his left leg over to clasp the right; then arches his back and compels surrender. L cannot bring his body up to relieve the pressure on the tender spot because V's legs keep him down.

Fig. 57—The Leg-lock lying down: Notice that L is held down by V's legs

Paralyzing the Leg

If V wants to be nasty, he can saw at the tender spot of L's leg with the edge of the forearm. L will find walking rather difficult for some hours after.

Faults

(1) Beginners clasp the leg too high up or too low down. It must be clasped just at the base of the calf.

(2) Beginners arch back without first getting a tight clasp of the leg; and their arm-edge slips away from the tender spot.

(3) Beginners forget to keep the edge of the arm against the leg. They press with the flat of the arm.

(4) Beginners do not get the proper cup-and-ball clasp of the hands. This clasp helps to give the right action on the leg.

Leg-Lock 3—The Splits

When **V** is in the straddle position on top of **L** it may happen that **L** allows his legs to remain idle for a moment with the knees bent close behind **V**'s back. **V** by a pretended attack on the neck may keep **L**'s attention occupied while his legs twine themselves into **L**'s legs. Then by pitching his body well forward and straightening his legs he can spread **L**'s knees apart until the strain on the hip-joints compels surrender.

Fig. 58—The Splits

CHAPTER XI
ARM-LOCKS

The object of attack is the elbow-joint. The human forearm cannot move freely in every direction about the elbow-joint. When pressure is put on the forearm to bend it out of its usual course, the elbow feels it acutely.

When **V** is in such a position that he can increase the pressure, if necessary, to a breaking-point, without **L** being able to move, then we say that **L**'s arm is locked. The elbow-joint is particularly sensitive, and a very slight pressure applied with discretion soon becomes un bearable to **L**; while a sharper pressure will affect **L** almost instantaneously.

In the principal arm-locks **L**'s upper arm is held firmly in position while the lower arm is being bent back beyond the straight. At the same time **L**'s body is prevented from turning to ease the strain.

Arm-Lock 1

This lock is shown in four movements in Figs. 59-62.

If **L** while falling keeps hold of **V**'s jacket with his left hand too long, **V** may seize the sleeve, pull **L**'s arm well up to him, and, as he pulls, advance his left foot close in to **L**'s armpit (Fig. 59).

V now falls back—his weight pulling always on the sleeve—clasps **L**'s wrist and (in the very act of falling) swings his right leg around over **L**'s head. **V** is careful to bend his knee sharply in falling, so that his body reaches the mats right up against his left heel. His right leg at that moment has settled itself down across **L**'s throat, and his legs squeeze **L**'s arm between them. **V** is then lying at right angles to **L**'s body (Figs. 61 and 62). **V** seeks to turn **L**'s wrist so that the thumb comes uppermost. He then presses the arm gently down, arches his back gradually, and so gains the power of curving **L**'s arm a good deal beyond the straight. **V** must be very careful not to do this with a jerk; and he must be on the lookout for **L**'s surrender.

Fig. 59—V has caught the arm while L was falling

Fig. 60—In reality V's leg would not have swung around until he had fallen nearly to the ground

Fig. 61—V at the moment he reaches the ground. He does not pause in this position, but falls back at once

Fig. 62—V about to arch his back and strain the elbow-joint

Pressure in direction away from thumb

The lock may be effective without keeping exactly to some of these details. **V**'s body may not be exactly at right angles to **L**'s: it may slope a little either way. But this gives **L** a better chance to wriggle out in time. Again, **L**'s hand may not be turned thumb-up, but, if it is not, **V** can merely put on the pressure in the direction away from the thumb.

One thing is absolutely essential—**L**'s arm must come well through between **V**'s thighs. Therefore, **V**'s body must lie as near **L**'s shoulder as possible.

This is difficult for a long-legged Englishman; his knee-joint is apt to be stiff and difficult to bend enough. He should help himself by getting his left foot well in, the toe under **L**'s shoulder-blade; and by a good pull on **L**'s sleeve force the knee to bend sharply and keep his body from falling away from **L**'s side. There must be no gap.

Remember, then, these points:

(1) Bring the body down against your own heel at **L**'s side: pulling in on the sleeve if necessary.

(2) Press the left leg against **L**'s arm so as to nip it tight.

(3) Press with the left hand in the direction away from the thumb.

(4) Arch your back so that your weight comes partly on **L**'s throat for the final lock.

Escape

L may escape when the lock is not done thoroughly.

(1) If **V**'s thighs do not pinch tightly, **L** may jerk his elbow-joint through.

(2) If **V**'s right leg does not hold him down well, he may throw it off or turn over.

(3) **L** should always be ready to roll quickly towards **V** the moment he suspects the lock is coming; and thus, to withdraw his elbow from danger.

Arm-Lock 2

This arm-lock is more generally useful than the last and easier to do correctly. The final position is shown in Fig. 63, which gives the lock for **L**'s right arm.   The lock is exactly the same as Arm-lock 1 except for this:

That the leg which was before bent at the knee is now straight out across **L**'s body and clasped to the other leg.

Fig. 63—V can let go of the jacket and use both hands at L's wrist. Sometimes V will clasp the wrist with his arm instead of gripping it

In this position **V**'s legs can clasp the arm near the shoulder so that the elbow-joint comes well through; **V**'s body can come well up against **L**; and when **V** straightens his clasped legs a little, the arm is very tightly nipped.

With the thumb up (or failing that, in the direction away from the thumb), pressure may be applied by arching the back slowly and carefully as before.

Opportunity

Various chances for this lock occur in groundwork . The lock comes best when **L**'s arm is straight, but this is not absolutely necessary. It may be enough if **L**'s upper arm is well away from his body, particularly if he is pushing with it so that it tends to straighten out when the resistance is removed.

A favourite position for trying this lock is from the straddle position on page 40.

V is in the modified straddle position of Fig. 64, or he comes to it from the standard straddle. **L**'s right arm is pushing at **V**'s throat.

Fig. 64—An opportunity for Arm-lock 2

Preparation

V works his left knee forward close under L's shoulder; his thigh then keeps L's upper arm out from the body.

Movement

V suddenly brings his right foot nearer to L and throws his weight over on to it. His left leg can then lift from the ground (thigh coming against L's upper arm) and circle around over L's head (keeping always a pressure on L's upper arm), as, with a push off the right leg, he returns his weight to the left and falls round at right angles to L into the position of Fig. 63.

During the swing round V has pinned L's wrist, either gripping it with his left hand or hugging it with his left arm.

At the moment he reaches the position of Fig. 63 V clasps his feet together; by straightening the legs he gets a very tight grip on L's arm. He can now, almost at leisure, press down L's arm in the direction opposite to the thumb, arch his back, and compel surrender.

This rather complicated movement is made in one piece, and in a very short interval of time. It is so important that it should be treated as an exercise and practised repeatedly until it can be done rapidly and effectively. Make a dummy figure with an arm to practise upon if your friends are unwilling. Notice that this arm-lock may be brought off from Hold-down 4, although if L keeps his hands clasped together it becomes the forced arm-lock (3).

Faults

1. The leg has to be swung round while the body is left to fall backwards, and beginners find it hard to do the two things together. They are not able to swing the leg round in one sweep because their balance is bad, and so they change the swing round into two awkward steps, the first of which gives warning to the man attacked.

2. Then, when they can swing the leg right round, beginners allow both legs to come up in the air at the finish of the sweep round, and so fail to grip the opponent's arm near enough to the shoulder. The important thing in arm-locks is to get the elbow-joint well through.

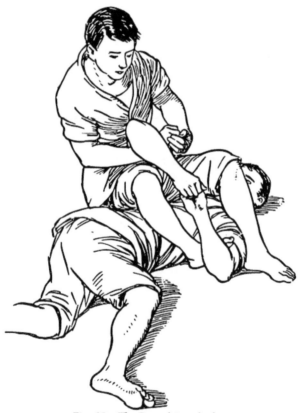

Fig. 65—The Forced Arm-lock

Arm-Lock 3—The Forced Arm-Lock

When **L** tries to prevent an arm-lock by clasping his hands together, the lock can be forced in this way.

V brings his legs round as before, one on each side of **L**'s right arm. As in Fig. 65, he passes an arm through **L**'s bent elbow and takes the ball of his fist in the cup of his other hand. He leans back with all his weight—driving the bony edge of his forearm into **L**'s biceps or into **L**'s bent wrist, as the case may be. He gets a purchase by placing a foot on **L**'s left upper arm and pushing with the leg.

It is impossible for **L** to resist this for very long; the dead weight of **V**'s body and the easy thrust with the leg soon tire out **L**'s fingers. **L**'s hands come apart; **V** falls back on the mats, shifting his right hand to **L**'s wrist and his left either to wrist or sleeve. **V**'s body is already well up against **L**: he has only to link his legs and finish the lock.

Opportunity

A fine chance for forcing an arm-lock comes when **V** is in the straddle position, if **L** rolls on one side. There is then more weight behind **V**'s fall, and a better purchase for **V**'s leg-thrust on the upper arm.

Fig. 66—Opportunity for V to catch L's right arm
in a One-leg Arm-lock

Arm-Lock 4—One Leg Arm-Lock

The previous locks require that **L** shall be lying on his back; the present one meets the occasion when **L** is facing downwards. He may be up on his hands and knees, or even half on his feet and over **V**, when the lock is put on him. Evidently then, this lock covers a quite new field of possible positions.

The conditions for the lock will be seen by considering an important example.

V is on his back in Standard Position II with his feet on **L**'s hips; **L** is either feeling for a neck-hold with his right hand or pushing at **V**'s throat. **V** brings **L**'s body lower, as in position (b), Attack 4, page 48, and proceeds to the attack.

Movement

First, he pins **L**'s right wrist (either by a grip or by hugging it with his arm), hitches his hips to the left, lifts his left leg over **L**'s head, and brings it across **L**'s right arm and back against **L**'s throat or face. Then turning on to his right hip he straightens the leg, arching his back at the same time. **L** collapses lower, and his arm is locked (Fig. 67).

Fig. 67—The One-leg Arm-lock

Notice that this is the same bend-back motion of the elbow-joint that is used in the first three arm-locks; here the straightening of the leg and the consequent forward thrust of the hip as the back is arched stretches the imprisoned arm at the elbow.

V must be careful to hold **L**'s hand high up on his chest. If it slips down, it may sometimes be pulled up again by the wrist and sleeve before the leg is thrown across. Otherwise the lock is apt to fail.

V must, then, remember:

1. To keep **L**'s wrist high up on his chest.

2. To hitch his hips strongly to the left.

3. To straighten his leg and arch his back for the final lock.

Here is an interesting example of this lock.

84

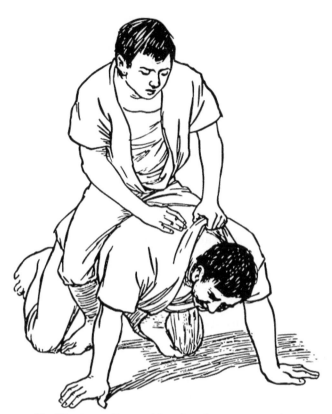

Fig. 68—A wrestling position that give an opportunity for the One-leg Arm-lock

An ordinary wrestler often gets in the position of Fig. 68 to avoid being turned on his back. Besides the neck-lock he is then exposed to a one-leg arm-lock.

For this **V** slides down to the ground on to his shoulder. While falling thus, he curls his right arm under **L**'s forearm. As his shoulder meets the ground, he hugs the forearm to his chest, throws his left leg over the arm, and (Fig. 69) brings it back against **L**'s face in the manner already described.

V may find it necessary to drop **L** nearer to the ground by pushing away **L**'s left arm with the unemployed foot. And also he may sometimes have to pull the arm to him by the sleeve.

In general, we may say that whenever **V** sees a straight arm, he should try to lock it, if he has a leg free to be thrown across **L**'s face.

Fig. 69—V can lower L's body by shoving away the supporting arm. In finishing the lock, V straightens his left leg and arches his back

Arm-Lock 5—Thigh-and-Foot Arm-Lock

In this lock **L**'s arm is not brought up to **V**'s body, as in all the preceding arm-locks. It is caught over the thigh and under the foot, and is possible from only one particular position—that of Fig. 70. The position for it is described as Hold-down 2, which may be reached without difficulty from Hold-down 1. In Fig. 71 **V** is lying across **L** with his left thigh pressed close up under **L**'s shoulder and his right leg nearly straight out. **V** has managed to catch **L**'s wrist with his right hand, and to straighten out the arm over his thigh. By slipping his left foot over the wrist he securely holds the arm down. **V** then lays his right leg on top of his right (as in Fig. 72), draws both legs (and **L**'s arm with them) somewhat backwards, and hoists a little with his left thigh. This makes the lock. It is often not necessary to use the second leg.

Fig. 70—Opportunity for Thigh-and-Foot Arm-lock

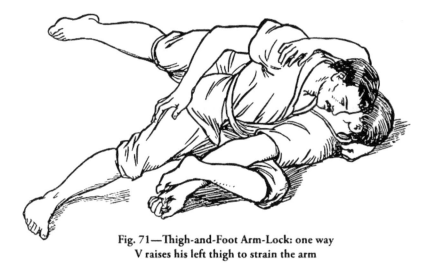

Fig. 71—Thigh-and-Foot Arm-Lock: one way
V raises his left thigh to strain the arm

The important thing in this lock is the position of **V**'s left thigh. It must be well under the shoulder, the knee projecting beyond the shoulder. Fig. 71 shows the correct position of the thigh. **L**'s arm must be brought across the thigh, well up near the hips, not near the knee. The arm is thus well raised in the air and prevented from sliding sideways when **V** draws it with his legs. It can be easily strained to breaking-point provided **L**'s body be kept down. Therefore, **V** must be careful to let plenty of weight rest on **L**'s body.

This lock depends on getting **L**'s arm out straight. There is a good chance of doing so, because **L** is afraid of keeping his arm too much bent on account of Arm-lock 6, the bent arm-lock that we shall now consider.

Fig. 72—Thigh-and-Foot Arm-lock
V draws his legs back for the final strain

Arm-Lock 6—The Bent Arm-Lock

L must be lying on his back.

There are several opportunities for this lock. For example, **V** may secure it from Hold-down 1. Fig. 73 shows how he seizes **L**'s left wrist, palm upwards, with his left hand at a moment when **L** is bending the arm. He then slips his right hand under **L**'s upper arm and clasps his own left wrist.

Now **V** levers up with his right arm, pressing against **L**'s upper arm from the purchase on his own left wrist. His left arm is pressing **L**'s wrist towards the ground, and the effect of the right-arm leverage is to draw **L**'s wrist round under the shoulder. This is the lock.

The same lock may be done from the straddle position. **V** passes his left arm under **L**'s neck, and clasps the wrist as before. This is not much good.

Note—It is important that **V** should turn the palm upwards when he first seizes the wrist.

Fig. 73—The Bent Arm-Lock
Notice that L's palm must be turned upwards

CHAPTER XII
ADVANCED THROWS

Hip-Throws

X throws you.

You were coming forward. **X** stepped his right foot (toe out) as near as possible right in front of you; at the same time, he began to slip his arm round your waist (Fig. 74). His arm came well round your waist as he brought forward his left foot, followed by the whole left side of his body. So, bringing forward his left side, he passed it through between his right leg (knee well bent) and your body (see Fig. 75), pivoting with his weight on the toes of the right foot, until his left foot came to the ground near his right, and both feet were pointing straight away from you.   His right hip was then right under you: his knees were well bent, as in Fig. 76. All this while he kept a firm pull on your left sleeve. Now straightening from the knees, he hoisted you in the air and let the sleeve-pull tilt you over his back to the floor (Fig. 77).

Fig. 74—Stepping in for Hip-throw

Fig. 75—This is really a picture for another kind of throw; but it shows very well how X passes his hip through

Fig. 76—X has his body well under you

Fig. 77—You fall over X's back when he straightens his legs

When you try, your action is faulty.

Faults

  (1) Your arm goes too high on his back. It goes in easier thus, but is no use for hoisting **X**'s body in the latter part of the throw.

  (2) You do not get close enough under **X**. There must be no gap between your bodies, or else **X** will merely slip down when you hoist.

  (3) You must not plant your feet apart, because then you cannot twist the hips well.

  (4) Even when your feet are near one another, you do not twist your hips through enough, and so your back is not well under **X**.

It is necessary:

  (1) To step in with toes pointing out, ready to pivot; weight on the toes.

  (2) To place the feet close together; they must point, at the end, straight away from **X**.

  (3) To keep well sunk down on bent knees until the final hoist.

  (4) To thrust the hips well through.

SIDE-THROW

X throws you.

X had been pulling you to his left. Then he suddenly began pulling you to his right and you planted your left foot rather firmly to resist this side-pull (Fig. 78). Immediately he put his left foot across in front of yours, twisted himself so as to face to your left (Fig. 79), and got a more forward downward pull on you in a direction in which you were not braced to resist (you had braced yourself against the original pull). So, your body came down and forward a little and your leg tilted up (Fig. 80), and **X** threw you over his leg by an easy screw of his shoulders.

Fig. 78—Opportunity for Side-throw   Fig. 79—First move for Side-throw

Fig. 80—X ought not be leaning forward like this. He could not keep steady for the photograph in the proper position

Faults

(1) You try from too far away. Your own pull bends you backwards into a very awkward position, and, besides, **X** has plenty of room to step over your leg.

(2) You get in the same awkward position because your left arm remained stiff with the elbow up, and of itself kept your body from coming close to **X**.

(3) Your position for the throw is too much in front of **X**. You should be more off to his side. **X** must trip over your lower leg; if you try to throw him over your hip, he will not upset over so high an obstacle.

(4) Your right knee remains turned in, and therefore you could not give the final screw with the body.

Remember, then:

As your body approaches X for the throw, your left elbow must come right in to your side and the palm of the hand must turn upwards.

Weight must remain well over your right foot, and right knee must be well bent.

Right foot must point well out, and so must the knee in order to allow the body to screw at the end of the throw.

Left leg must be kept straight.

Body must be kept straight. It must not lean forward, as in Fig. 80. (The man is leaning forward in that picture because he couldn't manage to keep   his balance otherwise while the photographer was messing about.)

This is a fascinating throw, but horribly hard to do in the hurry of contest, unless (by some happy accident) you get the time just right.

INSIDE KICK-BACK

X throws you, as in Figs. 81 and 82.

Fig. 81—The Kick-back from inside

Fig. 82—X hoisting your leg and pushing over your body

X was pulling you forward; and you came rather too close to him letting your weight come rather heavily on your left foot by way of bracing yourself against his pull. Just as your foot touched the ground X gave a sort of kick and lift blow behind your knee (Fig. 81) that for a moment weakened the leg and then drove it forward into the air. Your weight kept on coming on to the hoisted leg, you wanted to bring it down—making a long stride; but X (getting some purchase from his blow on your leg) pushed your

93

shoulders back with all his weight (Fig. 81), and you collapsed over your supporting knee, and fell.

It is very seldom that a proper opportunity for this throw will occur. You will often try the kick-and-lift blow, only to find that **X** had not really got his weight on the leg you kick, and that he easily lifts bis leg back.

Then again, you will often try too late, when **X** has already got his foot solidly planted on the floor, and the leg refuses to be kicked up.

CHAPTER XIII
APPARATUS

Space Required

In theory there is no limit to a Ju-jitsu ring; a contest might be fought out all over a ten-acre field with good results, and the field need not of necessity be flat. For practical purposes a contest has generally to be confined to smaller spaces; and for ordinary Ju-jitsu the space should be level. Hillside Ju-jitsu would need separate study.

Choose a space as large as possible; it is better not to have to make use of the walls. Confined-space Ju-jitsu is again a special art.

For a satisfactory Ju-jitsu contest a space twenty feet square is required. With good will, a fair game may be had in a space fifteen feet square; and much groundwork can be done in a room of half that size.

Space

There is considerable saving in the amount of space required when several couples are practising together. It is only occasionally that a couple wants much room. Thus, while one couple wants twenty feet square, two couples could do almost as well in the same space; for four couples or more, about 160 square feet of space per couple is enough. Each couple does not keep to its own little plot, but moves about freely as the contest requires, avoiding collision with the other couples just as it would avoid a pillar or wall. To make the most of the space in this way, there should always be some couples at groundwork, to give as much freedom as possible to those standing.

Mats

The ground-surface should be smooth, firm, and not too hard. Ju-jitsu mats are about 2½ inches thick of platted straw covered with matting, hard of surface, but springy. These mats are 6 feet by 3 feet, and simply laid down side by side. Their weight keeps them in place. At present they have to be imported from Japan and are expensive, costing 14s. each, landed in London. A space 18 feet square would cost £13 to furnish in this way.

Mats can be made in England of canvas stuffed with coconut fibre, which serve very well. They should be bigger than the Japanese mats, that there may be fewer joints. They must be quilted, to keep the edges full and square. They are softer than the Japanese mats—too soft and slow—and they get out of order. They are also expensive, costing from 1s. to 1s. 4d. per square foot.

We have known Ju-jitsu practised in a backyard on ordinary straw palliasses. If the game be played out of doors, nothing is better than thick turf, clear of stones. Canvas or a carpet may be spread over the grass to save wear.

A sandy beach will do very fairly, though it is not perfect. Sand is rather dead; there is no spring off it.

Taking thick grass turf as a standard, some tolerable makeshift can generally be devised for indoor work, and it is not necessary that everything should be perfect. There is as much fun in village cricket as in a match at Lord's. And Ju-jitsu, by its nature, should be adaptable to all circumstances.

The simple carpeted floor may be used by those with some skill in falling, but it is rather hard for the beginner. Very little is wanted to moderate the hardness—some thicknesses of matting, old blankets, straw, etc.—using always a canvas or carpet over all to give a smooth surface.

We know of a very successful practice-room where an old carpet has been strained taut by ropes going to rings inserted in the wainscoting, and pads of cheap sea-grass (varécque) laid beneath.

Clothes

The ordinary Ju-jitsu apparel consists of a pair of light shorts (no buckles), a light under-vest, or zephyr, and a jacket. The jacket, which alone calls for notice, is made with short sleeves and a padded collar. (The padding makes it more pleasant to grip.) Fig. 83 will make its construction clear enough.

A jacket should cost, at any tailor's, about 12s.

The game is usually played with bare feet, or an ordinary sock may be worn; or, better, if covering is really wanted on the feet, a sock made of some soft leather like a glove—a deerskin moccasin is excellent.

Footwear is only advisable when the surface is not perfectly smooth, and the toes liable to catch in the mats. The material must be decently smooth and soft, or the legs of the other man will suffer.

The jacket should be of the very strongest Irish linen duck, cut to the shape of Fig. 83. It is tied in with any kind of soft sash, preferably one 3 yards long of white sateen.

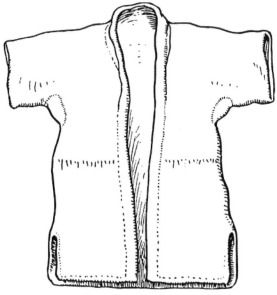

Fig. 83—A Ju-jitsu jacket

Special care must be taken to have the front edges of the jacket very firm, and the join of the sleeve must be strong and extremely well stitched.

The best sort of knickers are those made of strong cotton material, pulled in with broad tapes at the waist and below the knee.

Any kind of shorts or bathing-drawers will serve.

A long-sleeved vest should perhaps be worn beneath the jacket to prevent the galling of the neck and the skinning of the elbows on the mats.

For the guidance of the tailor, these measurements should be given:

(1) Length down the back (about 4 inches longer than for an ordinary coat).

(2) Size round the chest.

(3) Length from waist to just below knee.

(4) Length from fork to just below knee.

Just about to lock the arm
A fine opportunity for Arm-lock

CHAPTER XIV
THE JAPANESE SCHOOL OF JU-JITSU

Chief Instructors: Mr. MIYAKE, Mr. TANI, and Mr. HIRANO

Instructors: Mr. EIDA and Mr. KANAYA

Assistant Instructors: Messrs. COLLING RIDGE, McDONNELL, and HOBDAY

Instructor for Ladies: Miss ROBERTS

Time table

In general, it may be taken that the School is open for lessons from 9 a.m. to 9 p.m.

According to the hour of the day there are two or three or four instructors at work.

On the days when the School is undertaking demonstrations, some of the instructors may be withdrawn from teaching. Due notice of such temporary withdrawal is posted to pupils.

Advantage offered by the School

Apart from all question of the value and interest of the subject that it teaches, the School has set itself to supply a definite want. The School will be a place to which a man may go on any day and at any time that he feels the desire for exercise. He is tied down to no class hours, he need make no appointment. His course of lessons is subject to but a single condition, that it should be completed within a certain number of months.

Quick exercise for busy people

The busy person, the man with three-quarters of an hour to spare, the man who could just get in a lesson on his way to business or before catching an evening train—all these have but to ring up the School to secure in advance the lesson period they desire. And at the school they can change, have their fill of hard exercise, bathe, and depart within the short period of forty-five minutes.

When football and rowing must be given up

There are many people who groan that they can no longer spare time for the sports of their youth. Rowing, football, and open-air games mean a railway journey and the loss of an afternoon. Such people should do the next best thing and learn Ju-jitsu.

Am I too old to learn?

No. But after forty-one must expect to learn more slowly than at twenty-five.

Ju-jitsu can be made just as strenuous as one may desire, and pupils over seventy may well bear this in mind.

Ju-Jitsu for Children

For many parents Ju-jitsu has come a generation too late. They have the consolation, however, that they may play the game vicariously in the persons of their children, and parents who perceive the strong tendency that exists in the rising generations to be over-tall, to run to mere stalk, length without breadth, to be awkward and angular, should consider heavily (especially after reading this book) before they economise in the opportunities for their children's bodily development.

Courses of 12, 24, 39, 52, 78, 104, 156, 312 lessons respectively may be taken.

INSTRUCTORS OF THE JAPANESE SCHOOL OF JU-JITSU

MR. COLLINGRIDGE   MR. HIRANO   MR. MCDONNELL   MR. HOBDAY
                    MISS ROBERTS
       MR. KANAYA   MR. EIDA

How and When lessons may be taken

The lessons of any course may be taken on any days and at any time that the School is open. A pupil need give no previous notice of his intention to take a lesson. It is understood, naturally, that a pupil who arrives at the school without having secured a lesson period in advance takes the risk of having to wait until the instructors are disengaged.

Pupils may take two lessons a day if they so desire, or they may take two lessons running; but they will find the latter rather hard work.

DEMONSTRATIONS OF JU-JITSU

The School has already given a number of private demonstrations at such places as the Royal Military Academy, Woolwich, Eton College, Charterhouse, Chelsea Barracks, and at various club reunions, at various social festivities known as "at homes," and in the open air at garden parties in various parts of the country.

We would draw the attention of headmasters and of secretaries of clubs and of military and athletic associations to the fact that a demonstration of Ju-jitsu is not only interesting, effective, and highly genteel, but that it can also be counted upon to arouse a certain enthusiasm among spectators. It forms in effect a striking novelty in entertainment.

A pamphlet is published by the School giving the demonstration programme with full explanatory notes.

A full demonstration will occupy from one hour to an hour and twenty minutes.

A floor space of 20 feet by 20 feet is required for the mats.

A postcard to the Secretary will procure notice of public demonstrations given by the School.

Having beaten down the Leg Defence, the man (U) is getting hold for a Neck-lock